BUILT FOR REBUILDING

BUILT FOR REBUILDING

How to Rise When Life, Career, or Circumstance Falls Apart

First Edition

JOE CULLEN

Joe Cullen Ltd
Success Solutions Publishing

Published by Success Solutions Publishing, 2026
A Joe Cullen Ltd. Company

Interior Design: Creative Publishing Book Design

ISBN Paperback: 979-8-9947793-0-9
ISBN eBook: 979-8-9947793-1-6

For every person rebuilding a life after it broke apart.
For every person who has been dismissed, doubted, or overlooked.
For every person who deserves a second chance.
And for every rebuilder standing at the edge of a new beginning:

You are not alone, and this book is your proof.

"We may encounter many defeats,
but we must not be defeated."

— **Maya Angelou**

Table of Contents

PART I
The Breaking. When Life, Career,
Or Circumstance Falls Apart

PART II

The Calling. Why Built For Rebuilding Exists

PART III
The Center Pillar of Built for Rebuilding

Pillar 1: Dignity & Identity Restoration

PART IV
The Four Corner Pillars of Built for Rebuilding
Pillar 2: Truth & Clarity

Pillar 3: Tools & Skill Building

Pillar 4: Structure & Strategy

Pillar 5: Income & Stability

PART V
The System. How Built For Rebuilding Works

PART VI
The Reader's Rebuild.
How This Works For You

PART VII
Purpose & Impact. The Rebuild Beyond You

APPENDICES

Preface

I didn't build *Built for Rebuilding* because it sounded good. I built it because I lived the absence of it.

There are seasons in life when things don't just go wrong; they come apart. Not cleanly. Not all at once. Sometimes loudly and publicly. Sometimes quietly and alone. Sometimes in ways you never imagined were possible for you. I know those seasons well. I've lived them from more than one angle. As a founder. As a leader. As a husband. As a father. As a man whose identity fractured under pressure. As someone who learned the hard way that success does not protect you from collapse, and intelligence does not shield you from losing yourself.

When my life broke, what hurt most wasn't the loss of income, status, or momentum. It was the loss of identity. The quiet erosion of dignity. The slow disappearance of certainty. I didn't know who I was anymore, and I didn't know how to rebuild without pretending, performing, or becoming someone I wasn't. What I needed didn't exist.

- There were business books, but they assumed stability.
- There were self-help books, but they avoided reality.
- There were systems, but no compassion.
- There was motivation, but no structure.
- There was advice, but no lived understanding of collapse.

I didn't need inspiration. I needed a way forward that honored what I had survived.

Built for Rebuilding was born from that gap.

This book is not a theory. It is not a slogan. It is not a brand exercise. It is a system forged in lived experience, shaped by collapse, tested through rebuilding, and refined by walking alongside others who were trying to do the same. Every framework in these pages comes from real work with real people navigating real consequences, not hypothetical problems.

Through **Joe Cullen Ltd**, I work with entrepreneurs, professionals, and leaders who are rebuilding careers, businesses, and identities after disruption, burnout, or reinvention. Through **Sidre**, I work with justice-impacted individuals who are rebuilding their lives against barriers that most people never have to face. These are two expressions of the same mission. Different doors. One truth.

People don't fail because they lack effort. They falter because they lack dignity, clarity, tools, structure, and stability at the same time… This book exists to change that.

- I believe rebuilding should not require humiliation.
- I believe clarity should not come from shame.
- I believe accountability should not feel like punishment.
- I believe structure should support people, not suffocate them.
- I believe stability is not a luxury, it is a requirement for human flourishing.

Most of all, **I believe every person deserves the chance to rebuild a life stronger than the one that broke.**

If you are holding this book, you are not here by accident. Something in your life has shifted. Maybe quietly. Maybe violently. Maybe by choice. Maybe by force. You don't need to justify why you're here.

You don't need to explain your collapse. You don't need to prove anything to me. This book will ask you for honesty, not perfection. Engagement, not urgency. Courage, not bravado.

Read it slowly. Use what serves you. Leave what doesn't. Return to it when the season changes.

You are not broken... You are rebuilding.

And you do not have to do it alone.

— Joe Cullen

Acknowledgement

Keith Cheney, MA, LMFT

Much of this book would not be possible without the work and support of Keith. He has worked with me for years, helping me through the ups, downs, trials, and tribulations of my current rebuilding process. Most of the CBT experiences shared in the Built for Rebuilding™ program come from my time working with Keith. I had to acknowledge my appreciation for all that he does.

Author's Note

Before We Begin

I didn't write this book from a mountaintop. I wrote it from the valley; from the seasons when life collapsed in my hands, from the nights when I didn't know what tomorrow would look like, from the moments when my identity shattered, confidence eroded, and direction felt like something other people were allowed to have. This book wasn't created at a distance; it was built from lived experience.

There's a myth that rebuilding requires strength first, but that isn't true. Rebuilding begins with honesty. With admitting, "I don't know what comes next. I don't recognize my life right now. I'm tired. I'm scared." Strength is something we grow into. Truth is where we begin.

Before we step into this journey together, I want to offer you something I wish someone had given me when my own life fell apart: you don't have to be ready to rebuild; you just have to be willing. You don't have to feel strong. You don't have to have the plan. You don't have to know how to fix everything or pretend you're okay. You only need one thing: a willingness to take the next step, even if you can't yet see the whole path.

Dr. Martin Luther King Jr. once said that faith is taking the first step even when you can't see the entire staircase. The civil rights movement was built on that kind of courage. In a different but deeply personal way, this book is a guide for your own movement, your rebuilding movement, your opportunity to rebuild with dignity, clarity, and pride.

My purpose in writing this book is simple. I built 'Built for Rebuilding™' because I never want anyone to walk through a collapse alone. I want you to have the tools, clarity, structure, and dignity I didn't have when my own world fractured. This isn't a book about perfection or performance. It's a book about becoming, about returning to yourself, about rebuilding a life that can hold the weight of who you are now, not who you were before everything changed.

I don't need to know your entire story to know that if you're holding this book, something in your world has shifted, and you're searching, not for motivation, but for a way forward. So let me tell you what I know to be true: you can rebuild a life stronger than the one that broke, and you don't have to rebuild alone. As you move through these chapters, take what serves you, leave what doesn't, and make room for whatever truth rises in you along the way.

This is your rebuild.

I'm honored to walk it with you.

—Joe

Built for Rebuilding: How to Rise When Life, Career, or Circumstance Falls Apart

There are moments in life when everything you've built no longer holds. Sometimes the collapse is loud. A business fails. A job disappears. A marriage ends. A public mistake reshapes your future. Sometimes it is quiet. Burnout. Disillusionment. Loss of direction. A slow erosion of identity that no one else notices, but you feel every day. And sometimes it is systemic, imposed by forces larger than any individual, stigma, trauma, incarceration, aging, or a society that measures worth by output alone.

Collapse does not discriminate. It finds high performers and quiet strivers alike. It finds leaders, builders, caregivers, and dreamers. It finds people who did everything "right" and people who made mistakes they will carry forever.

What matters is not whether collapse happens. What matters is what happens *after*.

This book exists for the people standing in that space, the space between what was and what comes next. The space where identity

1

feels uncertain, confidence feels fragile, and the future feels unclear. It exists for those who are not looking for motivation, platitudes, or quick fixes, but for something sturdier. Something honest. Something that can hold weight.

Built for Rebuilding is not about starting over... It is about starting wiser.

Who This Book Is For

This book is written for four kinds of rebuilders, though their stories may look different on the surface.

1. It is for those rebuilding after disruption, when life changed without permission and the old path disappeared.
2. It is for those facing midlife reinvention, when the life you built no longer fits the person you've become.
3. It is for entrepreneurs at zero, standing at the beginning with vision but no clear structure.
4. It is for justice-impacted individuals rebuilding against barriers most people never see, let alone understand.

These rebuilders arrive through different doors. But they all walk the same internal path. Each is asking some version of the same questions: Who am I now? What is still possible? How do I rebuild without losing myself again?

This book is written to answer those questions without judgment or shame.

What This Book Is (and Is Not)

This is not a self-help book in the traditional sense. It will not tell you to "think positive," hustle harder, or manifest your way out of reality. It will not minimize the damage of collapse or pretend that rebuilding is easy.

This is a rebuild book.

It is a system for rising after life breaks, grounded in lived experience, not theory. It blends emotional truth with practical structure. Identity work with real-world tools. Compassion with accountability. Clarity with forward movement.

You will not find jargon here. You will find language that tells the truth. You will not be asked to perform strength. You will be taught how to rebuild it.

Why Built for Rebuilding Exists

Most rebuilds fail for the same reason: they focus on external change before internal repair. People chase jobs before restoring dignity. They seek strategy before reclaiming clarity. They rebuild systems without rebuilding the self. And when the internal foundation is fractured, no external structure holds.

Built for Rebuilding exists to reverse that order.

This framework was born from lived collapse and tested through real rebuilding. It grew through decades of entrepreneurship, leadership, failure, recovery, justice involvement, and walking alongside others navigating the hardest seasons of their lives. It exists because too many people are told to move on without being shown how to move forward.

This book exists because rebuilding should not require humiliation. Because accountability should not feel like self-punishment. Because dignity must come before stability. And because people deserve systems that meet them where they are, not where the world thinks they should be.

How This Book Will Help You Rebuild

This book is structured intentionally, because rebuilding requires sequence. You will begin by understanding the breaking, not to relive it, but to name it honestly. You will move into restoring identity and dignity, because nothing stable can be built without them. You will learn the Five Pillars of rebuilding: truth, clarity, tools, structure, and stability, and how they work together. You will be guided through practical pathways for rebuilding life, work, and income in ways that are sustainable. And finally, you will be invited to see rebuilding not just as survival, but as purpose.

Throughout the book, you will find exercises, reflections, and frameworks you can apply immediately. You are not expected to finish this book with answers to everything. You are expected to finish it with a direction, a foundation, and the belief that you can rise from here.

One Last Thing Before You Begin

◊ You do not need to be ready to rebuild to read this book.

◊ You do not need clarity.

◊ You do not need confidence.

◊ You do not need a plan.

◊ You only need honesty.

If you are willing to see your life as it is, without distortion or collapse, this book will meet you there. If you are willing to rebuild slowly, deliberately, and with dignity, this system will support you.

You are not behind. You are not broken… You are rebuilding. And this book is your guide.

PART I

THE BREAKING: WHEN LIFE, CAREER, OR CIRCUMSTANCE FALLS APART

The Fracture Point

There is a moment when you know your life has changed. Not because someone announces it, not because something explodes, but because something inside you shifts in a way you can't unfeel.

Every fracture point has a sound. For some people, it's a phone call. For others, it's a diagnosis, a breakup, a business failure, or a moment of self-realization so sharp it almost knocks the breath out of them.

For me, it was never just one thing. My breaking came in chapters.

But the first time I truly understood what collapse felt like… I was standing in the ruins of a company I had built with everything I had, realizing I no longer recognized the person who built it. And in that moment, I realized collapse isn't just something that happens to your life: it happens inside you.

The Loud Break

When you build something from the ground up, you convince yourself you can carry anything. Pressure, responsibility, long days, longer nights; that's the cost of growth. And when it works, when success starts to take shape, you believe momentum is permanent.

Until the day it isn't.

My company didn't fade out slowly. It didn't wither over time. It fell apart *fast*... loud, unmistakable, public. One day, I was steering a machine I had built from scratch. The next day, I was watching it collapse, unable to stop the fall.

There's a specific kind of silence that follows a loud collapse. It's not peaceful. It's not reflective. It's the silence of shock: the blank, echoing pause after the life you knew disappears.

I remember standing there, not with anger or panic at first, but with a disorienting sense of emptiness.

What now?

Who am I without this thing I built?

What do I do next?

The fracture had begun.

The Quiet Break

After the loud collapse, something else happened, something slower and quieter.

I wandered.

On the outside, it looked normal enough: coaching, consulting, working with businesses, doing what I'd always done. But inside, I was drifting.

There's a different kind of collapse that doesn't make headlines or force hard conversations. The kind that looks like "functioning." The kind that looks like you're handling things. The kind where you're still working, still smiling, still moving, but no part of you feels connected to the life you're living.

I've lived through that collapse, too.

It's subtle. It's quiet. It's the type of break that loosens your identity one thread at a time until you don't even notice how much you're unraveling.

This chapter of my collapse wasn't dramatic, but it was dangerous. When you start drifting inwardly, your sense of self starts dissolving. You stop recognizing the person you've become.

I kept going. But I wasn't really *building* anything. I wasn't really *becoming* anything. I was surviving with a fractured identity and calling it momentum.

That's another fracture point.

The Break That Shook Me to My Core

And then came the moment I never expected; the moment that changed everything.

A mistake. An incident so far outside my character that even I couldn't make sense of it. A moment that made me justice-impacted, a felon.

There's no softer way to say it: this break shattered me.

It was loud. Louder than the business collapse, louder than the drifting, louder than all the quiet moments of doubt and fear that came before.

It forced me to face truths I had not been willing to acknowledge. It forced me to confront the parts of myself I had ignored. It forced me into a kind of collapse that strips everything away: identity, confidence, certainty, pride.

What remained was a version of me I didn't know how to carry.

People imagine collapse as one event, one fall, one instant. But mine was a hybrid; an accumulation of loud and quiet, sudden and slow, internal and external.

A life can break in more than one way. Mine did.

The Unseen Breaks

After the loud moments, the public ones, the undeniable ones, came the quiet ones again.

Panic. Insecurity. The sense that everything inside me was rearranging faster than I could keep up. And underneath all of it was a mental health struggle I didn't yet understand. Not the kind that announces itself. Not the kind you can explain. The quiet kind. The kind that shifts the entire emotional landscape of your life without you noticing it until you're already standing in the wreckage.

These were the breaks no one else saw, the internal fractures that cracked my identity long before my circumstances confirmed it.

The Moment You Stop Pretending

Every rebuild has a beginning. Not the moment things collapse, but the moment you admit they have. I can tell you with complete honesty: the turning point in my rebuild wasn't the fall. It wasn't the consequences. It wasn't the losses.

It was the day I stopped pretending I was okay.

Pretending keeps you trapped in the life that's collapsing. Honesty frees you to build the next one. Your rebuild begins the moment you tell yourself the truth:

This isn't working.

I'm not who I want to be.

Something broke.

I need to rebuild.

The fracture point is not the end. It is the invitation.

If You're Standing in Your Fracture Point Right Now

I want you to hear me clearly: You are not failing. You are transitioning. You are not broken. You are becoming. You are not stuck. You are standing at a doorway; one that no one wants to reach, but one that every rebuilder eventually arrives at. And if you're reading this, you've already done something brave.

The fracture point is frightening because it is supposed to be. It marks the end of the life that no longer fits you and the beginning of the life you will build from here.

You do not need the full plan to begin. You do not need confidence. You do not need certainty. You only need one thing: *a willingness to take the next step, even when you can't yet see the path that follows it.*

And that is where we go next.

CHAPTER 2

My Story: Collapse in Public and in Private

E very rebuilding story has a beginning, but it rarely starts where people think it does. Mine didn't begin with the biggest failure of my life, or the loudest collapse, or even the moment I found myself in circumstances I never believed possible. It began years before that, in the quiet places where identity starts to crack long before anyone else sees the damage.

I've lived several different rises in my life, and I've lived just as many falls. Some were sudden and public; others were slow and invisible. If you've ever felt like your collapse didn't fit into a neat narrative, that it unfolded in pieces rather than as a single event, I understand that. My story is a hybrid of breaking points: fast and loud, slow and quiet, external and internal.

This is not the full story, which unfolds later, in the places where we examine rebuilding more closely to understand what it actually entails. This chapter is simply the truth about how the fractures formed.

The Rise Before the Fall

Before everything collapsed, I was building something big. I had launched my latest company from scratch, one that grew quickly, loudly, and with a momentum that felt unstoppable. We were producing major content, partnering with well-known organizations, and making our mark in a competitive industry. I poured myself into it with the intensity that only entrepreneurs truly understand. The long days, the endless decisions, the pressure, the responsibility, it didn't intimidate me. It energized me.

And when it worked, it felt like confirmation: I'm built for this. I'm capable. I'm winning.

It's a dangerous kind of confidence, the kind that whispers, *You can carry everything*. The kind that convinces you that the pace is sustainable and the success is permanent. Until the day you realize it isn't.

The Loud Collapse

The fall wasn't gradual. It was fast. Loud. And public.

A series of events and decisions, some within my control, some far outside it (the 2008 financial collapse), collided all at once. What I had built began to come apart faster than I could hold it together. I remember the feeling vividly: watching something I had poured years of my life into start slipping away, piece by piece, no matter how tightly I tried to grip it.

There is a specific kind of shock that comes when success turns to failure in full view of others. You don't just lose a business. You lose identity, direction, confidence, and reputation. The ground you were standing on gives way without warning. I remember the silence in the office the day after everything fell apart: the kind of silence that makes you realize something is truly over.

In that moment, I wasn't thinking about rebuilding. I wasn't thinking about lessons. I wasn't thinking about resilience. I was thinking about survival, and what it meant to face a level of loss and disappointment I had never experienced. But the collapse didn't end there. It simply changed shape.

The Quiet Collapse

After the public fall came a season that looked calm from the outside. I went back to what I knew. I coached founders. I helped businesses scale. I consulted. I stayed productive, useful, and helpful. It looked stable. It even looked successful. But inside, I was wandering. The loud collapse had shaken the external structure of my life. The quiet collapse began dismantling the internal one.

I didn't recognize it at first; it felt like drifting, a loss of anchor, a slow erosion of purpose. But a quiet collapse is still a collapse. It is the moment when your external movement no longer matches your internal direction. You're working but not building. Showing up but not connecting. Producing, but not progressing.

This was the season when I began losing parts of myself without realizing it. The confidence I once had. The clarity. The grounded sense of direction. No headline marks this kind of fall. No one asks questions. No one sees the fractures. But inside, you feel every crack.

The Collapse That Broke Me

And then came the moment that changed everything.

I had something happen, something that was entirely out of alignment with my character, my values, and the person I believed myself to be. I didn't see it coming, and I didn't understand myself

15

well enough to stop it. It was a moment that led to legal consequences and made me justice-impacted, a felon.

I won't sensationalize it in this chapter. Not because I'm hiding from it, but because collapse is never defined by a single event. It is defined by what that event does to your identity. For me, this was the loudest break of all. It forced me to confront my own humanity, my own fragility, and my own blindness to what unhealed internal fractures can become when you don't address them.

The shame, the aftermath, the fear, the isolation, these were not abstract concepts. They were daily realities. This break didn't just collapse my circumstances. It collapsed my sense of self. But even that wasn't the final fall.

The Mental Health Fracture

After the loud collapse came another quiet one, a mental health crisis, one I didn't understand at the time. It didn't announce itself dramatically. It was slow, subtle, and corrosive. Panic. Insecurity. Racing thoughts. Deep lows that felt impossible to explain. Highs that masked exhaustion.

Many rebuilders don't realize they're in a mental health fracture until long after it begins. For me, I had been carrying untreated mental health challenges for years without recognizing their impact. When combined with stress, shame, fear, and pressure, they became their own kind of collapse.

This part is important because so many rebuilders, especially men, leaders, entrepreneurs, and justice-impacted individuals, experience collapse in silence. The world teaches us to push through, power on, and keep moving. But collapse doesn't care about momentum. It demands honesty. And honesty forced me to acknowledge something

I had never considered: I wasn't just dealing with external events. I was dealing with internal fractures I had never healed, never named, and never addressed.

Rebuilding would require more than strategy. It would require identity work. It would require clarity. It would require tools. It would require structure. It would require stability. It would require the Five Pillars long before I had language for them.

Rebuilding Begins Here

This chapter is not the full story; that will come later, when we talk openly about identity, recovery, work, purpose, dignity, and the reality of rebuilding after collapse. My intention here is simple: *To tell you that I have lived the breaking. All of it: loud and quiet, sudden and slow, external and private.*

I have lived collapse in public. I have lived collapse in private. And I have lived the long, complicated road of rebuilding from both.

This is why Built for Rebuilding exists. Not as a theory, not as a brand, not as a slogan. But as a lived truth. You do not need to have my story to understand collapse. You only need to have survived your own. And if you are here, reading this, then you have. What matters now is not the fracture. What matters is what you will build from it.

In the next chapter, we'll explore the lessons collapse teaches us: the lessons I learned the hard way, and the lessons you may already feel rising inside your own life.

CHAPTER 3

What Breaking Teaches Us (If We're Willing to Listen)

Collapse has a way of stripping life down to its most honest parts. It removes the noise, the performance, the pretending, and the structures we used to hold ourselves together. What's left is the truth, the truth about who we are, what we believe, and what we've been avoiding. But collapse doesn't automatically teach us anything. Some people break and stay broken. Some people break and get bitter. Some people break and pretend they never did.

Breaking only teaches us if we're willing to listen.

When life fractures, we can either rush to rebuild the old structure... or, we can stop long enough to understand what the collapse is trying to reveal. These are the lessons breaking taught me: slowly, painfully, and sometimes more than once. They are also the lessons most rebuilders discover in their own way, in their own time, whether they realize it or not.

Lesson 1: Clarity Arrives When the Noise Is Gone

Before collapse, life is loud. Work is loud. Identity is loud. Expectations are loud. Success is loud. Breaking removes the noise. Not gently, but effectively.

When my business collapsed, when my identity collapsed, when my mental health collapsed, each break stripped away something I thought I needed. In that emptiness, something else appeared: clarity.

Clarity doesn't arrive as a plan. It arrives as truth. Truth about what mattered. Truth about what didn't. Truth about what I had been carrying that was never mine to carry. Truth about the person I was becoming, and the person I was pretending to be.

Collapse exposes what was already cracked. Listening is what reveals the clarity underneath.

Lesson 2: Identity Is the First Thing to Break and the Last Thing to Heal

Most people think collapse begins with circumstances. But long before anything breaks on the outside, something breaks inside. Identity cracks quietly. You lose confidence. You lose direction. You lose yourself in the role you play or the pressure you carry.

Identity breaks quietly because we're too busy performing to notice the cracks. By the time the public collapse happens, the private one has already been unfolding. This is why rebuilding can't start with strategy. It has to start with identity.

You can rebuild a business while your identity is still fractured, but it won't hold. You can start a new career while still carrying the shame of the old one, but it won't sustain you. You can create a plan with a broken sense of self, but you'll abandon it the moment life tilts again.

Breaking taught me this: **People don't fall apart because they lack strategy. They fall apart because they've lost themselves.**

The rebuild begins when identity begins to heal.

Lesson 3: The Hardest Truth Is Usually the Most Necessary One

I remember sitting alone in my truck after the collapse, realizing I had no idea who I was without the identity I had built. There were things I didn't want to face: the fears, the insecurities, the untreated mental health challenges, the decisions I made in moments of emotional overwhelm, the slow drift into misalignment.

Breaking forced me into honesty. Collapse puts you face-to-face with the truth you avoided. The truth about your patterns. The truth about your wounds. The truth about your coping mechanisms. The truth about your identity cracks. The truth about the weight you've been carrying alone.

It's tempting to rush past that truth. To rebuild quickly. To prove yourself. To jump into something new so you don't have to feel what the collapse revealed. But collapse teaches us something essential: **You can't outrun the truth. You can only delay it.**

The rebuild begins the moment you stop running.

Lesson 4: Breaking Removes What Was Never Built to Last

Not everything that falls apart was meant to stay standing. Sometimes, collapse is not punishment; it's protection. It removes relationships that drained us. It exposes habits that harmed us. It ends careers we were no longer called to. It interrupts identities that were built on pressure instead of purpose.

Breaking showed me how much I was holding together out of fear, obligation, momentum, and identity confusion. When those pieces fell, I finally saw how unstable they were. There is a strange relief in watching something fall that you were exhausted from holding together. Collapse didn't destroy the parts of me that mattered. It destroyed the parts I was never meant to build my life on.

When you listen closely, breaking reveals what was temporary… and what deserves to rise again.

Lesson 5: You Learn Who You Are in the Aftermath

Not during the collapse. After it. When the crowd goes home. When the noise fades. When the adrenaline dips. When the consequences settle in. That's when you learn who you are.

Do you isolate or reach out?

Do you numb or confront?

Do you rebuild or retreat?

Do you blame the world or take responsibility for your part?

Do you collapse inwardly or begin the slow work of rising?

Breaking revealed parts of myself I might never have seen otherwise, strengths I didn't know I had, weaknesses I had been ignoring, resilience I didn't understand, and wounds I had to acknowledge if I wanted to heal. Collapse teaches you your edges, the outer boundary of what you can endure, and your depths, the inner capacity you didn't know existed.

But only if you're willing to look.

Lesson 6: Rebuilding Requires Slowing Down Before You Can Move Forward

Breaking taught me something I resisted for years: **The rebuild cannot begin at full speed.** You cannot outwork collapse. You cannot outrun grief. You cannot strategize your way out of identity fracture. You cannot power through shame or confusion. You cannot "hustle" your way back to wholeness.

Rebuilding requires stillness before motion. Reflection before strategy. Honesty before solutions. The world celebrates fast comebacks, but fast comebacks often recreate the same collapse… Meaningful rebuilds are slow. Intentional. Steady. Aligned.

Everything I teach in this book rests on this truth: **Rebuilding requires going inward before you can move outward.**

Without that, you recreate the same life that collapsed, just with different scenery.

Lesson 7: Breaking Is Not the End; It's the Invitation

Breaking doesn't end your story. It asks you to write the next chapter differently. It asks who you want to become now. It asks what you truly value. It asks what parts of your old life no longer fit. It asks what you want to build that will actually hold. Collapse didn't end my life. It began the life I live today: the work, the purpose, the mission, the system, the platform. Breaking is not the final chapter. It's the doorway.

"The question now, the question this book will help you answer, is what you want to build as you walk through that doorway."

PART II

THE CALLING. WHY BUILT FOR REBUILDING EXISTS

CHAPTER 4

The Lived Truth
Behind the Manifesto

Not a slogan. Not a brand. A lived experience
turned into a system for others.

S ome people build frameworks from textbooks and theories. And
 then some people build frameworks from lived experience; from
the fractures, the failures, and the long nights of trying to make sense
of a life that no longer resembles what it once was.

Built for Rebuilding didn't begin as a business plan. It didn't begin
as a polished strategy. It didn't begin as a brand. It began as the map
I wished I had when I was trying to rebuild my life.

The manifesto that now anchors this platform was written in the
aftermath of collapse, in the places where honesty came easier than
pretense, and where the truth of what rebuilding really requires became
impossible to ignore.

This chapter is about that truth: **the lived reality that shaped
the philosophy behind the Five Pillars and the entire Built for
Rebuilding system.**

Rebuilding Isn't an Idea: It's a Reality You Survive

People often think of rebuilding as a moment of inspiration. A breakthrough. A clean slate. A dramatic turning point. That's not how rebuilding works.

Rebuilding is born in the places where you don't know what tomorrow will look like. It's born in the identity fractures no one sees. In the doubts, you don't say out loud. In the fear that you will never feel stable again.

The manifesto that became Built for Rebuilding™ came from those places, not from a conference room, not from a marketing meeting, not from a branding exercise, but from lived truth: **You can rebuild a life stronger than the one that broke… but only if the rebuild starts with dignity, clarity, tools, structure, and stability.**

The Five Pillars weren't invented. They were revealed.

The Manifesto Was Written After I Lost Everything Except the Ability to Rise Again

When my business collapsed…
When I drifted in quiet collapse…
When I became justice-impacted…
When my mental health cracked open…

I didn't write a manifesto. I searched for one. I remember sitting at my desk late at night, searching for something, anything, that could help me understand what was happening… Something to help me understand the collapse. Something to help me navigate the fog. Something to help me rebuild without shame. Something that spoke to both the external and internal rebuilding that had to happen.

Nothing fit.

Most "rebuilding" advice sounded like motivational posters. Most systems assumed you were already stable. Most frameworks ignored identity, trauma, shame, and the complexity of rebuilding a life after everything has fallen apart. So, I wrote the manifesto I needed: first for myself, and later for anyone walking a similar path. Not a celebration of collapse. Not a sugar-coated promise. Not a slogan designed to sell hope.

A declaration of lived experience.

Why the Manifesto Begins With Dignity

When you lose your business, your career, your reputation, your stability, or your freedom, the first thing to go is not your confidence… It's your dignity.

Collapse strips away the external structures that once told you who you were. Rebuilding demands you reclaim your identity without shame, without performance, without pretending. The manifesto begins here because I've lived this truth: **No rebuild holds if identity remains fractured.**

You can believe that I've tried; it didn't work. Finding your identity, your voice, is the first and most vital step to your rebuild. You can stack strategy on top of strategy, but if dignity does not return, none of it will matter. You won't believe in the rebuild you're trying to create.

The center of the system is not business. It is not an achievement. It is not success. It is the human being doing the rebuilding.

Truth & Clarity: The Parts Collapse Forces You to Face

I spent years trying to outrun the truth: the truth of the pressures I carried, the truth of patterns I ignored, the truth of untreated mental health challenges, the truth of decisions made from exhaustion rather than alignment.

Collapse forced me to confront all of it. Not with judgment. With reality. Truth & Clarity became a pillar because breaking taught me something that no business book ever did: **You can't rebuild your life while lying to yourself about the life you've been living.**

The manifesto doesn't protect you from the truth. It brings you to it so you can rebuild on solid ground.

Tools: Because Willpower Alone Doesn't Rebuild a Life

People assume collapse is followed by determination, a surge of motivation to start over. It isn't.

Collapse is followed by confusion. Fog. Shame. Fear. Overwhelm. Mental fatigue.

Motivation doesn't appear in that space. Tools do. Tools give you something to do when you don't know who you are. Simple tools. Clear tools. Tools you can use when your mind feels fractured and your confidence is low. Tools that help you function again. Tools that give you small wins. Tools that rebuild identity through capability.

The manifesto includes tools because lived experience taught me this: **You do not rise because you feel strong. You rise because you have something to hold onto.**

Structure: The Path That Keeps You Moving When Emotion Can't

In my own rebuilds, there were days when I couldn't rely on emotion. There were days when I didn't have clarity. Days when shame, fear, or exhaustion made decision-making feel impossible. Structure carried me. Structure gives you something predictable when everything else feels uncertain.

The Five Pillars became a structure not because I designed them, but because I noticed their pattern across every rebuild, I survived:

- *Identity returns first*
- *Then clarity*
- *Then capability*
- *Then direction*
- *Then stability*

It is not theoretical. It is lived.

The manifesto reflects the architecture of rebuilding as it truly unfolds, not as people wish it would.

Stability: Because Hope Without Stability Is Cruel

When people say, "reinvent yourself," they often leave out the part where rent is due, kids need care, court fines exist, employers discriminate, credit scores matter, and systems are designed to work against certain people.

A rebuild without stability is not a rebuild. It is a temporary rise followed by another fall. The manifesto includes stability because life taught me this: **People don't rebuild because they dream. They rebuild because they feel safe enough to try.**

Stability is the final pillar because it protects the rebuild from collapsing again.

The Manifesto Is Not Mine Anymore: It's Yours

When I wrote the manifesto, it was a private truth. A personal declaration. A reminder to myself that I could rise again. But over time, something shifted. I realized everyone who rebuilds walks through the same emotional terrain, the same emotional architecture, the same identity break, the same confusion, the same need for clarity, tools, structure, and stability. Even if the circumstances look different, every rebuilder walks through similar challenges.

My lived truth became a universal truth. That's when the manifesto stopped being mine alone. Now it belongs to:

- *The person rebuilding after personal collapse*
- *The midlife professional starting over*
- *The entrepreneur at zero*
- *The justice-impacted individual reentering society*
- *Anyone rising from something they thought would break them for good*

The manifesto is not a message. It is a map. It is not inspiration. It is an instruction. It is not branding. It is a lived experience that has turned itself into a system someone else can use to rebuild their life. And that is why it stands at the center of this book.

Because collapse is personal… but rebuilding is universal.

CHAPTER 5

The Four Rebuilders

Four different stories. One universal human arc.

W hen people talk about "starting over," it often sounds like a single experience: one category, one identity, one type of person. But collapse wears many faces, and so does rebuilding.

Through my own journey, through coaching founders, through working with people in the hardest seasons of their lives, and through rebuilding my own life more than once, I discovered something that changed the way I see the world: **There are four types of rebuilders… but they share one universal human arc.**

Different circumstances. Different entry points. Different forms of loss. But the same emotional journey. I've been each of these rebuilders at different points in my life; each of these rebuilders begins in a different place, but they all walk the same path:

Identity → Clarity → Tools → Structure → Stability → Rebirth.

This chapter introduces these four groups, not as "audiences," but as real human stories, each carrying their own weight, their own hope, and their own reason for beginning again. These four groups represent the most common entry points into the rebuild, but they are not the only ones.

1. The Rebuilder After Disruption

When life breaks in unexpected ways.

This rebuilder never planned on starting over. They weren't preparing for reinvention. They weren't searching for a new path. They were living their life, until something changed everything.

Maybe it was:

- Divorce
- Illness
- Burnout
- Depression
- Job loss
- Betrayal
- A family crisis
- A financial collapse
- The slow unraveling of a life that no longer fits

For the rebuilder after disruption, life fractures suddenly or subtly, pulling the rug from beneath them. They look around one day and realize: **The life I knew is gone. And the life ahead of me is unclear.** This group often struggles with identity the most. Not because they lack strength, but because nothing about this collapse was chosen.

Disruption forces questions no one ever expects to answer:

- *Who am I now?*
- *What do I do with what's left?*
- *How do I rebuild a life I never planned to rebuild?*

This rebuilder enters the system seeking direction, stability, and a new sense of self that honors what they've survived. They are not lost. They are beginning again.

2. The Midlife Rebuilder

The reinvention no one saw coming, including them.

This rebuilder is often in their 40s, 50s, or 60s. They've lived enough life to know who they are. They've built careers, families, reputations, rhythms… And then something shifts.

Sometimes the shift is external: a layoff, a company closing, an industry changing, or a business no longer viable.

Sometimes it's internal: a growing sense that the life they've built doesn't match the life they want.

The hardest part for the midlife rebuilder is not the collapse. It's the disorientation that comes after:

- *Am I really starting over at this age?*
- *What does reinvention look like now?*
- *Is it too late to become who I was supposed to be?*

Mid-life rebuilders often grieve not just what they lost, but who they were supposed to become. They grapple with grief for the old identity and fear of the new one. They carry responsibilities: mortgages, aging parents, children, bills, and the stakes feel higher than ever.

But midlife rebuilders also carry something powerful: Wisdom that wasn't available in their twenties. Clarity that comes from lived experience. And a willingness to rebuild with intention rather than speed.

Their rebuild isn't a comeback. It's an evolution.

3. The Entrepreneur at Zero

The builder before the building exists.

This rebuilder is different. They may not have experienced standard collapse; they're standing at the beginning, not the end. But they share the same uncertainty. The same identity questions. The same need for tools, clarity, and structure. Beneath the vision, there is often fear: fear of failing, fear of choosing wrong, fear of not being enough.

The entrepreneur at zero often enters the rebuild path because they feel something rising inside them: a vision, an idea, a business, a sense of purpose, but they don't yet know how to shape it.

Their questions sound like:
- *Where do I start?*
- *What am I actually building?*
- *How do I create something stable, not chaotic?*
- *What skills do I need that I don't have yet?*
- *Can I really do this?*

This rebuilder isn't coming from collapse; they're trying to **avoid** collapse. They want to build something sustainable, something aligned, something that stands the test of time rather than burning them out or breaking them down. Entrepreneurs at zero need: identity clarity, a simple strategic path, tools that reduce overwhelm, and a structure that keeps them grounded.

Their rebuild is forward-facing, building toward a life they haven't lived yet.

4. The Justice-Impacted Rebuilder

Rebuilding in a world designed to deny it.

This rebuilder carries a different weight.

A weight the world often refuses to see. A weight shaped by stigma, barriers, judgment, and systems built to punish long after the sentence is served. The justice-impacted rebuilder isn't just rebuilding a life; they're rebuilding their identity in a society that tries to define it for them.

Their questions are heavier:

- *How do I rebuild when doors are closed before I knock?*
- *How do I find stability when the system fights me at every turn?*
- *How do I trust myself again?*
- *Who am I beyond what happened?*

This rebuilder is navigating: Employment barriers. Housing discrimination. Financial limitations. Legal constraints. Mental health challenges. Family strain. Identity wounds. Shame that doesn't belong to them.

Their rebuild is not a personal project; it is an act of resistance. For them, rebuilding requires dignity, support, community, and a system that believes in their humanity. Their rebuild begins the moment someone treats them with dignity again.

This group is the beating heart of Sidre, and a core part of why Built for Rebuilding exists at all.

Four Journeys, One Human Arc

While these rebuilders have different stories, different pressures, and different reasons for beginning again, they share one undeniable truth: collapse, whether sudden or chosen, places every human being at the same starting point: **Who am I now, and what comes next?**

Each rebuilder must move through the same emotional and structural path:

1. **Identity work**: restoring dignity and sense of self
2. **Clarity work**: stabilizing thinking and direction
3. **Skill building**: gaining what collapse took away
4. **Structure building**: creating the path forward
5. **Stability work**: securing the future

The circumstances differ. The human arc does not.

This chapter introduces the four entry doors to the rebuilding system. But no matter where someone enters, they will walk the same internal path, guided by the same Five Pillars, toward the same outcome: A life rebuilt with purpose, stability, and dignity.

CHAPTER 6

Joe Cullen Ltd. and Sidre: A Dual Mission United by Purpose

How the for-profit and nonprofit arms serve the same rebuild journey. Why Sidre is the heart of the mission.

Peple often assume that a for-profit business and a nonprofit organization must have different goals, different identities, and different missions. But the truth is simple: both Joe Cullen Ltd. and Sidre were built from the same source: lived experience, broken seasons, and a calling to help people rebuild lives that have been fractured.

These two arms of the work look different from the outside. Different structures. Different audiences. Different funding models. Different responsibilities. But beneath those differences is one unifying truth: **Both exist to help people rise from collapse with dignity, clarity, tools, structure, and stability.**

Joe Cullen Ltd. is the strategic, educational, and advisory arm. Sidre is the community and support program for the justice-impacted. Two business models. One mission. Both are serving the same rebuild journey. I needed both in my own rebuild strategy. I needed the dignity, the structure, and the humanity that developing both entities provided on my journey.

The Origin Story: Why Two Entities Exist

Joe Cullen Ltd. evolved from decades of entrepreneurial experience: building five companies, scaling operations, guiding founders, coaching leaders, and helping people stabilize chaos and turn ideas into sustainable, thriving businesses. It was built from professional experience.

Sidre was built from something deeper. Sidre was born out of lived truth: the seasons of collapse where identity fractures, where the world becomes small, where systems become walls, and where a person must rebuild not just a career or business, but an entire life. Sidre emerged from the part of my story that cost the most, but also taught the most.

Joe Cullen Ltd. teaches people how to build, lead, and grow. Sidre helps people reclaim who they are so they can believe they're worthy of building at all.

Joe Cullen Ltd.: The Strategy and Structure of Rebuilding

Joe Cullen Ltd. serves the rebuilders who need:
- clarity of direction
- entrepreneurship as a path forward
- operational stability
- leadership frameworks
- decision-making tools
- business strategy
- personal operating systems
- mindset and identity alignment

It speaks to:
- the entrepreneur at zero
- the midlife rebuilder seeking reinvention
- the professional rebuilding after disruption

It uses:
- education
- advisory
- coaching
- courses
- systems
- frameworks
- writing and speaking
- Podcasts

Joe Cullen Ltd. helps rebuilders turn clarity into capability and capability into stability. This is where people learn the *how* of the tools, strategy, structure, and stability that allow the rebuild to hold. But not everyone can enter the next level of a rebuild from strategy alone. Some rebuilders need something deeper. Something more human. Something that meets them before the clarity arrives.

That space belongs to Sidre.

Sidre: The Heart of the Mission

Sidre is not just a nonprofit. It is the emotional, philosophical, and humanitarian core of Built for Rebuilding. Sidre exists to remind people that their story is not over.

Sidre serves the people rebuilding under the most difficult conditions:
- justice-impacted individuals
- people returning home after incarceration
- individuals living under stigma, restriction, and surveillance

- those navigating unemployment, homelessness, or financial instability
- those carrying identity wounds the world refuses to acknowledge

Sidre is the arm of the mission that says: **You have the right to rebuild. You have the ability to rebuild. And you will not rebuild alone.**

Sidre offers:

- dignity-centered identity restoration
- emotional support
- entrepreneurship pathways
- job readiness
- financial literacy
- mentorship
- community
- practical reentry tools
- housing support in the long-term vision

Sidre exists because collapse is not evenly distributed in the world. Some people fall farther. Some people fall harder. Some people fall into systems designed to keep them from rising again. Sidre was built to break that cycle.

A Shared Philosophy, Two Expressions of Service

Both Joe Cullen Ltd. and Sidre operate from the same core truth: **The belief that every person deserves a second chance and the tools to make it count.** But each serves different needs.

Joe Cullen Ltd. answers the question: *How do I build or rebuild my work, my business, my leadership, or my financial future?*

Sidre answers the question: *How do I rebuild myself when the world has already decided who I am?*

One teaches strategy. The other restores identity. Both are necessary. Necessary for everyone trying to rebuild. Without identity, strategy collapses. Without strategy, identity has nowhere to grow. Together, they form a complete rebuilding ecosystem. One restores the person. The other restores the path.

That ecosystem: Built for Rebuilding.

Why Do I Say: Sidre Is the Heart of the Mission

Because Sidre represents the part of the journey most people never see. The part where someone is deciding if they are still worthy. The part where shame and stigma weigh more than any business failure. The part where systems create barriers no one can climb alone. The part where the internal collapse is louder than the external one.

Sidre is where dignity is rebuilt first. The central pillar of everything Built for Rebuilding stands for is dignity.

Sidre is the reminder that rebuilding is not just a personal journey. It is a social one. A communal one. A justice one.

Sidre is the heart because:

- its people have the hardest road
- its mission carries the deepest purpose
- its work protects the humanity behind the system
- it embodies the truth that no rebuild is possible without dignity

Sidre ensures the mission stays honest: grounded not in theory but in lived experience, in compassion, in human worth.

Joe Cullen Ltd. ensures the mission scales: giving tools, strategy, and structure to rebuilders ready to rise.

Together, they form a dual mission with a single purpose: **Rebuilding lives, identities, careers, and futures with dignity, clarity, and a pathway forward.**

Two Roads, One Destination

Whether someone arrives through:

- collapse after disruption
- midlife reinvention
- entrepreneurship at zero
- or reentry after incarceration

...the rebuild begins the same way:

With dignity.

With truth.

With tools.

With structure.

With stability.

Wherever you enter this system, you will be met with what you need. This chapter exists to show you, the reader, something important: **You are not just entering a book. You are entering a system built from real experience, for real people, in real collapse.** And you will not walk that road alone.

CHAPTER 7

The Promise: You Can Rebuild a Life Stronger Than the One That Broke

You can do this, and you do not have to do it alone.

E very rebuild begins with a belief long before it becomes a plan. A belief that often feels fragile at first, sometimes so faint a person can barely hold onto it. This chapter is about that belief. Not motivation. Not positivity. Not inspiration for its own sake.

This chapter is about the *promise* that underpins the entire Built for Rebuilding philosophy: **You can rebuild a life stronger than the one that broke. And you do not have to rebuild it alone.**

This promise is not a slogan. It is not a marketing line. It is not the optimistic hope of someone untouched by collapse. It is a lived truth, earned through seasons where rebuilding felt impossible, invisible, or undeserved. Belief feels fragile because collapse teaches you to doubt yourself before anything else.

I built every tool, every program, every framework in this book on that single foundation: the belief that collapse is not the end of a story but the turning point of one.

The Philosophy Behind the Promise

Collapse doesn't just break you; it breaks you open. Rebuilding is not about bouncing back. It is not about returning to who you were before the collapse. You cannot unbreak what broke you, and you were never meant to. What you are meant to do is rise as someone wiser, more grounded, more aligned, and more capable than before.

The philosophy behind this promise rests on three truths:

1. Collapse strips away what was never stable.

When life breaks, the pieces that fall were already fragile, identity built on external validation, systems built on overextension, relationships built on imbalance, and careers built on old versions of ourselves. Collapse exposes what no longer serves us.

2. Rebuilding reveals who we truly are.

When everything unnecessary is stripped away, we see the truth of what remains. Our values. Our resilience. Our capacity. Our character. Our direction. Collapse does not erase identity; it clarifies it.

3. Strength is a product of alignment, not force.

The strongest rebuilds are not fueled by willpower alone but by honesty, dignity, clarity, and structure. Strength is created when a person is finally aligned with who they really are, not who they were pretending to be.

- **This philosophy is why the Five Pillars exist.**
- **It's why Sidre exists.**
- **It's why Joe Cullen Ltd. exists.**
- **It's why this book exists.**

Because rebuilding is not just possible, it is predictable when the right system is in place. You deserve a place where rebuilding is not questioned but expected.

The Belief System That Makes Rebuilding Possible

Built for Rebuilding is grounded in a belief system shaped by lived experience, not theory. A belief system that says:

- **People deserve second chances.**
- **People deserve dignity.**
- **People deserve tools.**
- **People deserve clarity.**
- **People deserve structure.**
- **People deserve stability.**

Rebuilding begins when a person accepts these truths:

1. **You are not broken beyond repair.** Your collapse does not define your worth.
2. **Your story is not over.** This chapter is not the final one; it is the hinge.
3. **Your identity is not lost.** It is waiting for you beneath the rubble.
4. **Your life can still be rebuilt: intentionally, steadily, beautifully.** Not perfectly. Not instantly. But truthfully.

For the person who feels stuck…

For the person who feels ashamed…

For the person who feels too old, too late, too lost…

For the person who feels forgotten…

This promise is your beginning.

The Emotional Truth Under Every Tool and Framework

Every strategy in this book, the identity work, clarity exercises, tools, systems, and stability practices, rests on a deeper emotional truth: **Rebuilding is not just a process. It is a return to self.**

47

◊ Before you rebuild a plan, you rebuild a person.

◊ Before you rebuild a business, you rebuild belief.

◊ Before you rebuild a future, you rebuild the foundation of who you are.

People do not fail at rebuilding because they lack strength. They fail because they lack **structure, support, and a system that sees them as human first.** That is the heart of Built for Rebuilding. It is not about hustle. Not about grinding. Not about pretending everything is fine.

It is about:

• Restoring dignity in a world that often strips it away.

• Rebuilding identity after life fractures it.

• Creating clarity where confusion once lived.

• Gaining tools that remove overwhelm.

• Building structure that turns survival into progress.

• Securing stability that makes growth sustainable.

The emotional truth is this: **People rise when they are met with compassion and given a clear path forward. Not one or the other. Both.**

The Promise You Must Accept Before You Begin

You may not know exactly how to rebuild yet. You may not feel ready. You may still be carrying shame, fear, uncertainty, or exhaustion. None of that disqualifies you from a rebuild. The only requirement for rebuilding is this: **A willingness to believe that a different future is possible. Even if you don't yet know how to reach it.**

Every chapter that follows serves one purpose: to show you how to turn that willingness into structure, step by step, pillar by pillar.

If you're reading this, you've already done something brave. You are not reading this book by accident. You are here because something in your life has shifted, and you are searching for a way forward. Let this chapter be the moment you accept a truth that will carry you through the rest of this journey: **You can rebuild a life stronger than the one that broke. And you are not doing it alone.**

In the next chapter, we begin to rebuild together.

PART III

THE CENTER PILLAR OF BUILT FOR REBUILDING

Pillar 1:
Restoring Dignity, Agency, and Inner Direction

CHAPTER 8

When Identity Breaks: The Hidden Fallout of Collapse

Collapse doesn't just rearrange your circumstances. **It rearranges you.** It cracks the parts of your identity you thought were solid, exposes the pieces you didn't know were fragile, and shakes the foundations you didn't realize you were standing on. When life falls apart, whether loudly in public or quietly in private, the most profound damage rarely appears on the outside.

The real breaking happens internally.

There's a moment after collapse when people look in the mirror and don't fully recognize the person looking back. Not because they have changed physically, but because something deeper has shifted: the sense of who they are, what they are capable of, and what their life is supposed to mean. This is the hidden fallout of collapse: the identity break most people never talk about. This chapter is where we begin to name it.

How Collapse Fractures Identity

When life is steady, identity feels stable. We know our role. We know our rhythm. We know the story we tell ourselves, and the story others believe about us.

Then something happens:

A divorce.

A job loss.

A business failure.

A burnout that slowly eats away the edges.

A legal consequence that changes everything.

A health crisis.

A quiet unraveling that no one notices.

Suddenly, the story shifts. The rhythm breaks. The role disappears. And with it, the identity attached to it. Identity doesn't only break when something catastrophic happens. It breaks when the meaning we once attached to ourselves no longer fits.

Collapse fractures identity in three ways:

1. **It disrupts who we believed we were.** The achiever. The parent who held everything together. The provider. The leader. The strong one. The stable one. The person who didn't make mistakes. When that identity cracks, it feels like losing a part of your foundation.

2. **It exposes who we fear we might be.** Not enough. Not worthy. Not capable. Not redeemable. Not who we thought. This fear, not the collapse itself, is what keeps so many people stuck.

3. **It forces us into a version of ourselves we never prepared for.** The one starting over at 50. The one navigating the legal system. The one rebuilding after a mistake. The one

unemployed, unsure, or untethered. The one grieving a version of life that no longer exists. Identity fractures because identity was built, in part, on external structures that collapsed.

What Identity Collapse Feels Like

People often expect a collapse to feel dramatic: like a landslide or a lightning strike. But identity collapse is often quiet, subtle, and deeply personal. It sounds like:

"I don't know who I am anymore."

"I don't trust myself right now."

"I feel like everything about me changed."

"I don't know what I'm supposed to do next."

"I don't want anyone to see me like this."

"I can't believe this is my life."

Identity collapse has symptoms, even if you don't notice them at first:

- You question decisions you used to make easily.
- You second-guess your own value.
- You feel disconnected from your sense of purpose.
- You hesitate to take steps you once took confidently.
- You feel like an outsider in your own life.
- You stop dreaming because dreaming feels unsafe.

This is also where the body reacts. Identity collapse doesn't just live in the mind; it shows up in the body as:

- Tension
- Fatigue
- Restlessness
- Numbness
- A heaviness you can't explain.

55

The body often feels the fracture before the mind understands it. It is the psychological disorientation of losing the internal map that once guided you. And here is the part many rebuilders struggle to admit: **Identity collapse can feel like grief.** Because in many ways, it is. Not grief for a person, grief for a version of yourself that is gone.

Why Identity Breaks First Before Anything Else

We often think that collapse destroys our circumstances first. But what collapses first is the story we tell ourselves about those circumstances.

◊ A job loss is not just a job loss. It is a threat to identity: "Who am I without this role?"

◊ A divorce is not just the end of a relationship. It is a fracture in identity: "Why wasn't I enough?"

◊ A legal consequence is not just a sentence. It is an assault on identity: "Does this define me now?"

◊ Burnout is not just exhaustion. It is identity erosion: "Why can't I be who I used to be?"

Identity breaks first because identity is the part of us that gives meaning to everything else. When the meaning changes, the self-changes.

Why the First Rebuild Is Internal, Not External

Most people try to rebuild by fixing the outside: Get a job. Start a business. Move somewhere new. Find a new partner. Take on a project. Work like hell to make something happen. But external rebuilding without internal rebuilding creates instability. It's building a house on ground that hasn't settled yet.

You can rebuild your circumstances quickly. You can rebuild your identity only honestly.

The first rebuild, the non-negotiable rebuild, is internal:

- Restoring dignity
- Reclaiming identity
- Regaining agency
- Reestablishing self-trust
- Reconnecting to worth

Until these pieces are rebuilt, nothing external truly holds. Every person I've ever coached, mentored, or walked alongside has eventually discovered the same truth: **The rebuild doesn't begin when your life changes. It begins when *you* change.**

Identity Is Not Who You Were. Identity Is Who You Are Becoming.

Identity collapse feels like loss, but it is actually a transition. A violent, painful, disorienting transition, but a transition, nonetheless. The person you were is gone. The person you are becoming is not yet formed.

Collapse creates a space between identities. A void. A silence. A moment when nothing feels solid. Most people fear this space. This often appears as shame. A shame based on their perception of what they think the world thinks of them. Shame is often the quietest but most corrosive part of identity collapse. They try to rush through it, fill it, avoid it, or numb it.

But this space, this identity in-between, is where rebuilding truly begins. This space requires patience, even when everything in you wants to rush. Because in that space, you finally have room to ask:

- *Who am I now?*
- *What matters now?*
- *What do I want to build from here?*
- *What parts of me need to be restored, not replaced?*

Identity is not about returning to the person you were. It is about becoming the person you are meant to be after everything changed.

The Hidden Gift of Identity Breakage

No one wants to collapse. No one chooses identity fracture. But there is a truth many rebuilders discover only in hindsight: **When identity breaks, it makes space for something more honest to emerge.** Identity doesn't just break alone: it breaks in relation to the people and systems around us. Collapse removes what was never truly yours. It exposes what was borrowed, inherited, or performed. It strips away what was built for survival, not alignment.

And in that stripping, something becomes possible: A rebuild not based on who you were expected to be, but on who you actually are. This is why identity restoration forms the center pillar of the entire Built for Rebuilding system.

It is not the first pillar because it sounds good. It is the first pillar because without it, nothing else stands.

Where We Go From Here

In the next chapter, we explore the forces that shaped (and misshaped) your identity long before collapse, the systems, stories, and seasons that taught you who you were allowed to be. Understanding those forces is the key to reclaiming your identity on your own terms.

The rebuild continues. And it begins with truth.

CHAPTER 9

The Forces That Shape Us:
How Systems, Stories, and Seasons Rewrite Identity

Identity doesn't form in a vacuum. It is shaped, and often misshaped, by the world we move through, the systems that define our choices, the stories we inherit, and the seasons of life we survive.

By the time collapse hits, most of us have been carrying identities built from forces we never consciously chose: family expectations, cultural pressures, workplace norms, trauma patterns, survival mechanisms, and the invisible architecture of society itself.

When identity breaks, it's not just the circumstances of collapse that cause the fracture. It's everything that came before it. Everything that shaped the self you're now trying to rebuild. Identity is not one story; it is the accumulation of every force that shaped you, whether you chose it or not.

This chapter explores the forces that influence identity long before collapse, because you cannot rebuild yourself until you can see the forces that built you in the first place.

Trauma: The Silent Architect of Behavior and Belief

Trauma doesn't always look dramatic. Sometimes it's not a single moment at all, it's a pattern, a season, a childhood dynamic, a series of relational injuries, or a long-term erosion of safety and self-trust. Trauma teaches you to protect yourself even when you no longer need protection.

Trauma reshapes identity in three ways:

1. It redefines what you believe is possible.

Trauma teaches people to lower expectations, minimize needs, and assume disappointment.

2. It distorts self-worth.

Trauma tells you that you must earn love, earn stability, earn belonging.

3. It creates survival versions of you.

- Hyper-independent.
- Hyper-productive.
- Hyper-vigilant.
- Hyper-resilient.

These versions served you once, but collapse reveals what they cost.

Trauma doesn't just hurt… It shapes. Rebuilding requires naming those shapes so they can be reshaped.

Stigma: The Identity Imposed From the Outside In

Stigma is identity theft. It replaces who you are with who the world decides you must be.

People who experience divorce, job loss, financial hardship, chronic illness, mental health struggles, or justice involvement all face stigma: spoken or unspoken.

Stigma says:

"You are defined by what happened."

"You are less than."

"You are your mistake."

"You are your collapse."

For the justice-impacted, stigma becomes systemic. It shows up in employment barriers, housing discrimination, social judgment, and the way people rewrite your identity without ever knowing your story.

Stigma is one of the heaviest forces shaping identity because it tells you that you must rebuild not only yourself, but your place in the world.

Culture: The Invisible Script We're Handed at Birth

The most powerful cultural messages are the ones we don't realize we absorbed.

Culture gives everyone a script:

- Be strong.
- Be independent.
- Be successful.
- Don't fail.
- Don't rest.
- Don't disappoint.
- Don't ask for help.

Depending on where and how you grew up, that script may be wrapped in:

- religious expectations
- gender roles
- community norms
- racial identity
- Southern resilience

- Midwestern stoicism
- immigrant survival instincts
- masculine suppression
- family legacy

Culture shapes identity long before you're aware of it. Collapse often shatters the cultural script, forcing you to ask: *What part of this identity was mine? And what part was inherited?*

Expectations: The Versions of You the World Required

Every person carries expectations, some imposed, some internalized.

- Be the reliable one.
- Be the achiever.
- Be the strong one.
- Be the fixer.
- Be the one who doesn't break.
- Be the one everyone counts on.

Eventually, the expectations others placed on you become the expectations you place on yourself. They define how you build your careers, families, and reputations. But they can also build cages.

When collapse happens, the "expected self" is the first thing to fall apart. That loss feels like failure, but it's actually liberation, the beginning of rebuilding the *authentic* self.

Justice-Impacted: When Systems Redefine Identity for You

Justice involvement forces a person into an identity they didn't choose. The system writes a label. Society reinforces it. Employment, housing, finances, and relationships are all reshaped by a single moment that becomes a lifelong weight.

For the justice-impacted rebuilder, collapse is not a single event. It is a series of systemic barriers that continue long after the sentence ends.

This identity distortion is so powerful that it can convince people: *"This is who I am now."*

But it is not. It is a system's narrative, not your identity. Rebuilding requires reclaiming the truth of who you are beneath the label.

Aging: The Quiet Identity Shift No One Prepares For

At midlife, identity undergoes a natural fracture point:

- Careers plateau or collapse.
- Children grow up.
- Bodies change.
- Dreams evolve.
- Priorities shift.

People expect youth to be the uncertain season, but the deeper identity crises often come at 40, 50, 60... Aging rewrites identity by asking the questions:

Is this still who I want to be?

Is this still the life I want?

Is it too late to change?

Did I miss my chance?

Rebuilding at midlife is not a reinvention of self; it is an alignment with a truer version of yourself.

Burnout: The Slow Disappearance of the Self

Burnout doesn't break identity suddenly. It erodes it quietly. You don't realize you're losing yourself because you're still functioning:

- Still working.
- Still providing.

- Still performing.
- Still pushing through.

Burnout rewrites identity by replacing *"who you are"* with *"what you can produce."* By the time collapse becomes visible, burnout has often been shaping identity for years, shoot… sometimes decades.

When worth is tied to output, rest feels like failure. Rebuilding requires separating your worth from your output, a process that feels uncomfortable for high achievers but is freeing once embraced.

Family Systems: The First Identity Teachers

Family systems create the earliest frameworks of identity:
- Who you're supposed to be.
- What emotions are acceptable.
- What success looks like.
- What failure means.
- What role you fill.

Every family creates identity dynamics:
- The peacemaker.
- The achiever.
- The responsible one.
- The golden child.
- The invisible child.
- The caretaker.
- The scapegoat.

Even in loving families, these early roles shape adulthood, affecting decisions, relationships, careers, and the way we respond to collapse. Rebuilding identity requires differentiating the *family role* from the *authentic self.*

Capitalism as an Identity Engine

In modern culture, capitalism does more than shape economics: it shapes identity. Your worth becomes tied to:

- productivity
- income
- status
- performance
- output
- visibility
- success narratives

When collapse disrupts your ability to produce, capitalism interprets it as failure, and people internalize it. This is why so many rebuilders feel shame after losing a job, closing a business, or stepping back from productivity:

- They weren't just losing income.
- They were losing identity.

Your worth is not your title, your paycheck, or your quarterly earnings report. Rebuilding requires reclaiming worth from something deeper than work.

Identity Was Shaped Before the Collapse. Now You Get to Shape It Intentionally

The forces above shaped you:

- Some strengthened you.
- Some distorted you.
- Some protected you.
- Some wounded you.

But identity built from outside systems is not identity built from truth. Collapse, for all its pain, gives you something unexpected: A chance to rebuild who you are without the weight of old scripts, expectations, traumas, or labels.

This chapter is not about blaming the systems that shaped you. It is about seeing them clearly, so they no longer control the rebuild.

CHAPTER 10

Self-Worth Is Not Optional

R ebuilding yourself is not an abstract idea. Rebuilding doesn't begin with a plan, a job, a strategy, or a new opportunity. Rebuilding begins with you.

Before the external rebuild can take shape, the internal rebuild must take root. Every pillar, every tool, every framework in this book rests on one truth: **A person cannot rebuild a life they do not believe they deserve.**

- **Identity fractures during collapse.**
- **Dignity is what erodes.**
- **Agency is what dissolves.**
- **Direction is what disappears.**

You can fix external circumstances, but if the internal identity is still fractured, everything remains fragile.

This chapter teaches you how to rebuild yourself slowly, practically, compassionately, and in a way that can hold your future. This is the work that allows everything else to stand.

The work begins in six areas:

1. **Dignity restoration**
2. **Agency regrowth**
3. **Identity reframing**
4. **Personal operating principles**
5. **Internal stability**
6. **Connecting self-belief**

These six areas form the internal architecture of the rebuild. They are not steps you complete once; they are practices you return to throughout your life. We will not just explore what these mean. You will learn how to practice them.

Section 1: Dignity Restoration

Why Dignity Comes First

Dignity is the foundation of the Five Pillars because it is the foundation of the self. Without dignity, rebuilding feels impossible because you do not believe you are worth rebuilding. Dignity restoration is the process of reclaiming your inherent worth after seasons, systems, and stories have stripped it away. Without dignity, people do not rise:

- They survive.
- They cope.
- They endure.
- But they do not rebuild.

Dignity is not pride. It is not confidence. It is not swagger or performance. Dignity is not a feeling; it is a posture you practice until it becomes truth. Dignity is the quiet knowing: **"I am still worthy of a future."**

Collapse convinces people otherwise. Shame convinces people otherwise. Stigma, trauma, culture, family systems, expectations, burnout, all work together to shrink identity into what the world has taught you to believe.

Rebuilding dignity requires three practical steps.

Step 1. Naming the Worth That Collapse Tried to Erase

- You are not your collapse.
- You are not your worst moment.
- You are not your lost job, your failed business, your broken marriage, your mental health crisis, or your legal record.

Dignity returns when you stop confusing identity with circumstance. Dignity begins with the statement: **"What happened is not who I am."**

Practice: The Identity Separation Exercise

Each morning, write this sentence and finish it:

"I am not ___; I am ___."

Examples:

- "I am not my past. I am the person learning from it."
- "I am not my collapse. I am the person rising from it."
- "I am not my burnout. I am the person reclaiming my strength."
- "I am not my record. I am a person determined to restore my life."

This simple practice begins to rewire identity at a subconscious level.

Step 2. Releasing the Shame That Does Not Belong to You

Shame is often inherited or imposed. It is rarely accurate. Dignity grows when you challenge the narratives placed on you, especially the ones you never chose. Shame can come from:

- Culture
- Family

- Stigma
- Systems
- Expectations

Practice: The Shame Audit

Write down:

1. The beliefs you feel ashamed of
2. Where each belief came from
3. Whether that belief is actually true

Examples:

- "I shouldn't be struggling." This came from culture. This is not a true statement.
- "A real man doesn't need help." This came from childhood. This is not a true statement.
- "I am defined by my record." This came from the legal system. This is not a true statement.

Shame loses power when it is named.

Step 3. Allowing Yourself to Take Up Space Again

Rebuilders often shrink after collapse. You speak less. Ask for less. Expect less. Hope less. The first act of dignity is expansion, the willingness to exist without apology.

Dignity is not a reward. It is a birthright. Reclaiming it is the first step of every rebuild.

Practice: The "Small Expansion" Rule

Every day, do one thing that asserts your right to exist:

- Speak up in a conversation
- Say "I need help"
- Ask a question
- Stand tall when you feel like folding

- Take a break without apologizing

Small expansions rebuild dignity internally.

Section 2: Agency Regrowth

Reclaiming Your Power to Act

Agency is your ability to make choices that shape your life. Collapse replaces agency with helplessness. Agency is the belief: **"I have influence over my own life again."**

Collapse steals agency. It replaces action with reaction. Choice with limitation. Movement with paralysis. Restoring agency does not start with big decisions. Agency often returns before confidence does. It starts with the smallest possible move:

- A choice you make intentionally.
- A boundary you enforce.
- A need you acknowledge.
- A truth you admit.
- A step you take because *you* chose it, not because the world demanded it.

Agency grows through three core practices.

Step 1. Micro-Decisions That Rebuild Self-Trust

Ask yourself:

> *"What do I need today?"*
> *"What can I choose right now?"*
> *"What is within my control in this moment?"*

Practice: The 1-Choice Rebuild

Every morning, choose: **"What is one thing I will choose today, not collapse?"**

Examples:
- "I choose to take a walk."
- "I choose to apply for one job."
- "I choose to drink water instead of skipping meals."
- "I choose to tell the truth instead of pretending."

Small decisions create momentum. Momentum creates confidence. Confidence creates new possibilities. One small choice per day rebuilds self-trust.

Step 2. Reclaiming the Right to Choose Your Direction

Agency is not power over the world around you. It is power *within* the world around you. You may not control all circumstances, but you can choose how you move within them.

Practice: The Options Inventory

List:
- 3 things you *can* do today
- 3 things you *could* do this week
- 3 things you *might* be able to do this month

They do not need to be big. They just need to be real. Agency grows when possibilities become visible.

Step 3. Shifting From Reaction to Intention

Rebuilders often wait for clarity before acting. But agency develops through movement, not perfection. Every rebuild requires this shift: From **"What will happen to me?"** to **"What can I choose next?"**

Practice: The Pause

Before making decisions, pause for 5 seconds and ask: **"Am I reacting… or choosing?"** This one question changes the posture of your life.

Section 3: Identity Reframing

Becoming the Person You Are After the Collapse

Identity reframing is not about "finding yourself." It is about rebuilding yourself on truth instead of survival, expectation, or performance. It begins with three questions:

1. Who was I before the collapse, and which parts were true?
2. Who am I now, in the aftermath?
3. Who am I becoming, if I rebuild intentionally?

Step 1. Who Was I Before the Collapse and Which Parts Were True?

Not all of your past identity was authentic.

- Some of it was inherited.
- Some of it was scripted.
- Some of it was survival.

These old scripts were shaped by culture, family, trauma, and expectations.

Examples:

- "I must always be the strong one."
- "I'm not allowed to fail."
- "My worth is in my productivity."
- "I must never show weakness."

Practice: The Script List

Write down every identity statement you were taught or absorbed. Next to each one, write: **"Does this still serve me?"** Most will not. Those that do not serve you become material for release in your rebuild.

Step 2. Who Am I Now, In the Aftermath?

Collapse reveals:

- What matters
- What doesn't
- What healed
- What hasn't
- What needs to change

Ask yourself:

- "Who am I now?"
- "What matters to me now?"
- "What version of myself feels most true?"

Practice: The 6 Identity Pillars

Write one sentence for each:

1. What do I value now?
2. How do I want to show up emotionally?
3. How do I want to handle conflict?
4. How do I want to love people?
5. How do I want to lead (even myself)?
6. How do I want to rebuild without pretending?

These become your new identity anchors.

Step 3. Who Am I Becoming, If I Rebuild Intentionally?

Identity reframing requires grieving the version of yourself you can no longer be. But you cannot stay there. You've decided you want to regain control of your life. That's the promise of this book; the promise you made to yourself by continuing to read. Identity reframing is a forward process, not a backward search. You are not returning to a former self. You are building a future self. Identity reframing allows you to say: **"I am no longer defined by what broke me. I am defined by what I choose to build next."** Identity is not discovered. Identity is designed.

Practice: The Becoming Statement

Complete this sentence:

"I am becoming the person who…"

Examples:

- "I am becoming the person who honors my limits."
- "I am becoming the person who rebuilds slowly but steadily."
- "I am becoming the person who gives myself dignity."

Identity reframing turns collapse into evolution.

Section 4: Personal Operating Principles

The Internal Framework That Holds You Steady

Before strategy comes stability. Before stability comes structure. Before either comes the internal operating system that guides your decisions, your behavior, and your emotional posture. Your personal operating principles are:

- The boundaries you set
- The truths you live by
- The expectations you release
- The values you choose intentionally
- The standards you hold yourself to
- The behaviors you reinforce
- The stories you refuse to carry forward

Personal operating principles turn emotional overwhelm into grounded clarity. Rebuilders need an internal compass. Not to limit them. To anchor them.

Step 1. Define Non-Negotiables

These are the lines you no longer cross with yourself.

Examples:

- "I don't rush decisions anymore."
- "I no longer make myself small."
- "I do not abandon myself."
- "I rest before I break."
- "I ask for help when I need it."

Practice: Write 5 Personal Principles

Write five "I" statements that reflect who you are committed to being now. These become your internal guardrails.

Step 2. Define Your Emotional Operating Principles

These govern how you relate to your own emotions and the emotions of others.

Examples:

- "I speak from calm, not panic."
- "I allow myself to feel without judgment."
- "I practice truth daily."

These principles turn emotion into alignment instead of chaos.

Step 3. Define Your Behavioral Operating Principles

These govern how you move through your days.

Examples:

- "I finish what matters, not everything."
- "I delegate what doesn't need my energy."
- "I choose sustainability over speed."

These principles become the foundation for the external rebuild that comes later in the book.

Section 5: Internal Stability

Creating the Conditions Where Growth Can Hold

Stability is built slowly, and that slowness is a strength, not a flaw. Internal stability is not emotional perfection. It is internal grounding. It means:

- You don't make decisions in chaos.
- You don't collapse under someone else's story about you.
- You don't spiral when external circumstances shift.
- You can stay steady enough to make progress.

Internal stability is built through four core skills:

1. Emotional regulation
2. Nervous system awareness
3. Thought clarity
4. Behavioral consistency

Self-belief is then rebuilt on top of that stability.

Step 1: Emotional Regulation

What it means: Emotional regulation is the ability to respond instead of react. Collapse often leaves people in a state of hyper-reactivity. Small triggers feel massive. Decisions feel pressured. Emotions dominate thinking. Rebuilders must learn to create space between the feeling and the action. This is not avoidance... It is control.

Practice: The 90-Second Rule

Emotions often peak for about 90 seconds. When you feel triggered, overwhelmed, embarrassed, or panicked:

1. Pause for 90 seconds.
2. Breathe slowly.

3. Name the emotion: "I am feeling ___."

4. Let the wave pass before you act.

This simple practice prevents emotional decisions and restores internal grounding.

Step 2: Nervous System Awareness

Your nervous system carries the weight of collapse, stress, trauma, mental health struggles, and chronic pressure. When your nervous system is overloaded, thinking clearly and rebuilding steadily becomes almost impossible. You cannot rebuild if you are constantly in fight, flight, or freeze.

Practice: The 3-Breath Reset

Take:

- Three slow breaths in through the nose
- Hold briefly
- One long, slow exhale through the mouth

Do this before:

- Job applications
- Difficult conversations
- Decision-making
- Triggering situations

Stability begins with the nervous system. You have to protect it. You can support it by:

- Prioritizing rest and sleep
- Moving your body regularly
- Practicing simple mindfulness or breathing
- Limiting constant crisis input (news, drama, chaos)

Step 3: Thought Clarity

What it means: Collapse distorts thinking. You begin to catastrophize, assume the worst, personalize everything, or predict failure before trying. Thought clarity is the ability to examine your thoughts instead of accepting them as truth.

It helps you:

- Organize your thinking
- Reduce mental fog
- Make better decisions
- Communicate more clearly
- Stay grounded in the present
- Align choices with your values

Practice: The Thought Check-In

When a painful or anxious thought appears, ask:

1. "Is this a fact or a fear?"
2. "What evidence actually supports this thought?"
3. "Is there another explanation I haven't considered yet?"
4. "What would I tell a friend if they had this same thought?"

Write the answers. Seeing your thinking on paper creates distance and clarity. This practice retrains the mind toward grounded truth.

Step 4: Behavioral Consistency

A rebuilder needs thoughts and actions that are stable, predictable, and reliable over time.

What it means: Identity and self-belief grow from small repeated actions… Not breakthroughs. Not big wins. Not perfect days. It's consistency.

Behavioral consistency:

- Makes you predictable to yourself
- Builds trust with others
- Aligns actions with values
- Creates a steady pattern of movement forward

Every small action becomes evidence that you are capable, stable, and rebuilding.

Practice: The Evidence Journal

Every night, write:

"Today I proved to myself that I can ___."

Examples:

- "…stay calm during stress."
- "…finish something I started."
- "…tell the truth."
- "…set a boundary."
- "…move forward even when uncertain."

Small evidence becomes deep belief. Stability is not the absence of struggle. It is the presence of tools that help you withstand it.

Section 6: Self-Belief Reconnection

The Final, and Most Difficult, Restoration

Building self-belief is a journey. It involves mindset shifts, intentional actions, and steady self-care. Self-belief is not confidence. Confidence fluctuates. Self-belief is deeper. Self-belief is the quiet, steady conviction: **"I can build something meaningful from here."**

After a collapse, self-belief often disappears. Not because people are weak, but because collapse convinces them they are incapable, unworthy, or permanently broken. Rebuilding self-belief requires practice.

Step 1. Challenge Your Negative Self-Talk

The internal voice that constantly criticizes you is a major drain on self-belief.

- **Catch the critic:** Notice negative thoughts as they arise.
- **Question the thought:** Is this based on fact, or just fear and habit? Would I say this to a friend?
- **Reframe with compassion:** Replace "I can't do anything right" with "Everyone makes mistakes; I can learn and do better next time."

Step 2. Set and Achieve Small, Achievable Goals

Success builds confidence. Start small to create a positive feedback loop.

- Break big goals into smaller steps
- Complete one small step at a time
- Celebrate each win, no matter how minor

Each completed step reinforces: **"I can follow through."**

Step 3. Take Care of Your Body

Your physical state impacts your mental state.

- Move your body regularly
- Eat in ways that fuel you
- Protect your sleep
- Shower, groom, and dress in ways that help you feel presentable

These are not vanity. They are signals to your brain that you matter.

Step 4. Step Outside Your Comfort Zone

Self-belief grows when you prove to yourself that you can handle more than you thought.

- Face small fears on purpose

- Treat failures as feedback, not verdicts
- Try new things: a class, a group, a hobby, a skill

Every new experience becomes a vote in favor of your capacity.

Step 5. Build a Supportive Network

The people around you shape the way you see yourself.

- Spend more time with people who support your growth
- Spend less time with people who constantly pull you down
- Ask for help when you need it — from friends, family, mentors, or professionals

You do not need to rebuild alone.

Practice: 30-Day Self-Belief Building Action Plan

Building self-belief requires consistent, small actions over time. This 30-day plan focuses on daily habits that shift your mindset, challenge negative beliefs, and build momentum through small wins.

Phase 1: Awareness & Mindset (Days 1–10)

Goal: Understand your current self-talk and establish gentle, positive routines.

Day	Action/Focus	Task
1	Awareness	Notice your self-talk. Just observe when you criticize yourself.
2	Gratitude	Write down 3 things you are genuinely grateful for.
3	Physicality	Take a 15-minute walk outside. Focus on your posture as you walk.
4	Challenge Talk	Identify one negative thought. Ask: "Is this a fact or just a feeling?"

Day	Action/Focus	Task
5	Self-Care	Dedicate 30 minutes to something relaxing (bath, reading, music).
6	Positive Input	Listen to a motivational podcast or watch an inspiring video.
7	Review Wins	List 5 things you accomplished this week, however small.
8	Body Image	Look in the mirror and give yourself one genuine compliment.
9	Limit Negativity	Unfollow 1 social media account that makes you feel "less than."
10	Affirmations	Choose one affirmation (e.g., "I am capable") and say it 5 times.

Phase 2: Action & Small Wins (Days 11–20)

Goal: Take small, deliberate actions to build a track record of success.

Day	Action/Focus	Task
11	Goal Setting	Write down one tiny, achievable goal for tomorrow.
12	Achieve Goal	Complete the goal you set yesterday.
13	Step Outside Comfort	Start a 2-minute conversation with a cashier, barista, or neighbor.
14	Learn Something	Spend 20 minutes learning a new skill online.
15	Review & Plan	Review your progress. Plan one focus for the next week.
16	Physical Activity	Try a new type of movement for 10 minutes (yoga, stretching, etc.).

Day	Action/Focus	Task
17	Say "No" Nicely	Politely decline one non-essential request. Protect your energy.
18	Seek Feedback	Ask a trusted friend for 2 things they appreciate about you.
19	Practice Posture	Sit or stand with strong posture for 30 minutes total.
20	Mindfulness	Do 5 minutes of quiet breathing or mindfulness.

Phase 3: Resilience & Consolidation (Days 21–30)

Goal: Solidify new habits and build resilience against setbacks.

Day	Action/Focus	Task
21	Forgiveness	Acknowledge one past mistake and choose to forgive yourself.
22	New Challenge	Set a slightly bigger goal (e.g., finish a book chapter).
23	Complete Challenge	Achieve the goal you set yesterday.
24	Visualize Success	Spend 5 minutes picturing yourself succeeding at a major goal.
25	Help Others	Do one act of kindness for someone.
26	Journaling	Write about a time you overcame a difficult situation.
27	Reward Yourself	Do something you genuinely enjoy as a reward for your consistency.
28	Support Network	Reach out to a supportive person just to connect.

Day	Action/Focus	Task
29	Future Self Letter	Write a letter to your future, confident self.
30	Reflect & Plan	Review the 30 days. Decide one habit you will keep going.

You Are the First Rebuild

Everything you build from this point forward, your business, your career, your relationships, your stability, your purpose, rests on the foundation of a rebuilt self.

The collapse did not ruin you. It revealed you.

It stripped away inherited scripts, survival identities, expectations, roles, and narratives that never truly fit. This chapter marks the end of **PART III The Center: Dignity & Identity Restoration**, and the beginning of the structural rebuild in **PART IV**.

You are now ready for:

- **Truth**
- **Clarity**
- **Tools**
- **Structure**
- **Strategy**

But none of those external tools work until you cultivate dignity, reclaim your agency, solidify your identity, establish stability, and embrace self-belief.

PART IV

THE FOUR CORNER PILLARS OF BUILT FOR REBUILDING

Pillar 2:
Truth & Clarity

CHAPTER 11

Telling the Truth About Your Life

Seeing what is real without distortion or collapse.

Truth is not a personality trait… It is a practice. And for a rebuilder, it is one of the most important practices you will ever learn. Not truth as in perfection. Not truth as in brutal honesty used like a weapon. Not truth as in "tell everyone everything."

Truth as in clarity. Truth as in reality. Truth as in being willing to look at your life as it is… without distortion, without denial, and without collapse.

Because rebuilding cannot begin on a lie. And it cannot hold on a story you keep editing to survive it. This is why Pillar Two matters: **Truth & Clarity.**

◊ Dignity restored you.

◊ Agency gave you motion.

◊ Now truth gives you footing.

◊ It is the moment you stop negotiating with reality.

◊ The moment you stop living inside the fog.

◊ The moment you stop confusing what you fear with what is real.

Truth does not crush rebuilders… Truth stabilizes them.

The Two Lies Rebuilders Live Inside

Most rebuilders don't lie in obvious ways. They don't wake up planning to deceive themselves. They lie in two subtle ways that feel like coping.

Lie one: Minimizing.

"It's not that bad."

"It's fine."

"I'm good."

"It'll work out."

"I've been through worse."

"I don't want to complain."

Minimizing is how you stay functional. It's how you keep showing up. It's how you avoid the weight of the truth. Minimizing often feels like a sign of strength… but it's actually a form of self-abandonment. By minimizing, you delay the rebuild, because you cannot solve a problem you won't name.

Lie two: Catastrophizing.

"My life is ruined."

"I'll never recover."

"I'm too far behind."

"I messed everything up."

"I'm done."

Catastrophizing is the other kind of distortion. It is when your nervous system writes the story. When fear becomes fact. When collapse becomes your identity.

Both distortions are trying to protect you. Minimizing protects you from pain. Your body reacts before your mind interprets. Catastrophizing protects you from disappointment. But neither one builds stability. Rebuilding requires a third option.

Clear truth.
- Not inflated.
- Not minimized.
- Not dramatized.
- Not denied.

Just real.

What Truth Actually Means in a Rebuild

Truth is not "everything is my fault." Truth is not self-blame. Truth is not shame. Truth is the ability to say:
- This is what happened.
- This is what it cost me.
- This is what is real right now.
- This is what I can control.
- This is what I cannot.
- This is what I need next.

Truth is a stabilizer. It ends the constant cycle of re-living. Re-explaining. Re-arguing with what already happened. Truth lets you stop fighting the past and start building the next step.

Why We Avoid Truth

Most people avoid truth for a simple reason. Truth feels like consequence.

"If I admit I'm burned out, I might have to change how I work."

"If I admit this relationship is broken, I might have to face loneliness."

"If I admit my finances are unstable, I might have to confront hard decisions."

"If I admit my identity is fractured, I might have to do deeper work than I planned."

Truth forces action. That is why we delay it. But here is the reality.

- Action is coming anyway.
- Time will demand it.
- Life will demand it.
- Your nervous system will demand it.

Truth just lets you choose the timing. And choose it with dignity.

The Rebuilder's Clarity Framework

"What's True, What's Real, What's Next"

This is one of the simplest tools in the Built for Rebuilding system. When life feels overwhelming, when your mind is spinning, when you feel stuck, you do not need a perfect plan. You need a clear inventory.

Step 1: What's True

Real is not punishment; it's orientation. Truth is the sentence you can say without defending it.

Examples:

- "My business is not stable right now."
- "I'm functioning, but I'm not okay."
- "I'm not who I was, and I don't know who I'm becoming yet."
- "I'm carrying shame that does not belong to me."
- "I don't trust myself the way I used to."

Truth is what you would say if you were alone in a room and could not perform.

Step 2: What's Real

Real is what exists whether you like it or not. Your current resources. Your current limitations. Your current responsibilities. Your current reality.

Examples:

- "I have two bills due this week."
- "I have support available, but I have not asked."
- "I have skills, but I am out of rhythm."
- "I have a record, and that will affect my options."
- "I have time, but I have been wasting it in fear."

Truth is internal. Real is external. You need both.

Step 3: What's Next

Next is not the 12-step plan. Next is the *next step*. Not what you can do when you feel better. What you can do now.

Examples:

- "Today I will make two calls."
- "Today I will ask for help."
- "Today I will write down my expenses."
- "Today I will set one boundary."
- "Today I will go for a walk and clear my head."
- "Today I will tell the truth to one trusted person."

Rebuilding moves at the speed of the next step. Not the perfect strategy.

Practice: The Truth Inventory

15 Minutes. No Drama. No Collapse.

Set a timer for 15 minutes. Write the answers to these prompts, clean and simple.

1. What am I pretending not to know?
2. What am I exaggerating because I'm scared?
3. What part of my life is unstable right now?
4. What part of my life is stable, even if it's small?
5. What is one truth I need to admit out loud?
6. What is one practical next step I can take in the next 24 hours?

This is not therapy. It is clarity. And clarity is one of the most compassionate gifts you can give yourself.

Seeing Your Life Without Collapse

Some people think truth is heavy. It can be. But distorted living is heavier.

- Carrying denial is heavy.
- Carrying panic is heavy.
- Carrying a story you don't fully believe is heavy.
- Carrying shame is heavy.
- Carrying ambiguity is heavy.

Truth is often the first moment you breathe again. Not because everything is fixed. But because your mind stops spinning. Truth creates stillness. And in stillness, you can finally see.

The Difference Between Truth and Harshness

Truth is not cruelty. A rebuilder does not need a voice that says:
"I screwed everything up."
"This is my fault."
"I should have known better."
"I'm behind."
"I've wasted time."
That is not truth. That is punishment. Truth sounds different.
Truth says:

- "This is where I am."
- "This is what I did."
- "This is what happened."
- "This is what it cost."
- "This is what I learned."

- "This is what I will do now."

Truth is clean.

- It does not add insult.
- It does not layer shame.
- It does not require you to hate yourself to change.

Truth creates clarity. Clarity creates agency. Agency creates motion. Motion creates stability. That is the rebuild sequence.

The First Honest Sentence

If you do nothing else after reading this chapter, do this. Write one honest sentence about your life right now. Not poetic. Not dramatic. Not polished... Just honest.

Examples:

- "I'm tired of surviving."
- "I don't trust myself yet."
- "I need structure."
- "I'm overwhelmed and I've been hiding it."
- "I'm ready to rebuild, even if I'm scared."
- "I need help."

That first honest sentence is not weakness. It is the beginning of the rebuild. Because the rebuild does not begin when you feel ready. It begins when you stop lying to yourself about where you are.

Closing: Truth Is the Doorway to Clarity

You cannot rebuild your life with a false map. Truth is the doorway. Clarity is what you see once you walk through it. Telling the truth about your life is one of the most courageous acts of rebuilding. And when you begin telling the truth about your life, something changes.

- You stop living in fog.

- You stop carrying stories that aren't true.
- You stop collapsing inside uncertainty.

You begin building from what is real.

In the next chapter, we're going to take this further. Because telling the truth is not just about naming reality. It is about learning how to see your patterns clearly, without shame, and without distortion. That is where clarity becomes power. And that is where the rebuild begins to accelerate.

CHAPTER 12

Clarity Without Shame

Accountability without self-punishment.
Honesty without self-attack.

C larity is not the same thing as harshness. And honesty does not require cruelty. Most people were taught that honesty is something you survive, not something that supports you. Many people avoid clarity not because they don't want the truth, but because they're afraid of what the truth will do to them. Somewhere along the way, truth became tangled with punishment. Accountability became synonymous with shame. Self-reflection turned into self-attack. So people stay foggy on purpose:

- They avoid naming what's broken.
- They soften facts.
- They tell partial stories.
- They stay busy instead of being honest.

Not because they're dishonest people, but because every time they've tried to look clearly, it came with pain. This chapter is about untangling that. Because clarity is not meant to harm you. Clarity is meant to stabilize you.

Why Shame Blocks Clarity

Shame distorts perception. It doesn't sharpen insight. It narrows it. When shame is present, the mind does one of three things:

- It **minimizes** ("It's not that bad.")
- It **catastrophizes** ("Everything is ruined.")
- It **personalizes** ("This proves I'm broken.")

None of those leads to the truth. They lead to avoidance, panic, or paralysis. Shame keeps you focused on *who you are* instead of *what is happening*. It turns information into identity. It turns data into judgment. And when clarity feels like a verdict, people stop asking honest questions. Rebuilding requires a different posture.

The Difference Between Accountability and Self-Punishment

Accountability asks: **What happened, and what needs to change?**
Self-punishment asks: **What is wrong with me?**

Accountability is forward-facing. Self-punishment is circular. Accountability creates options. Self-punishment creates weight. Accountability honors your dignity; self-punishment erodes it.

You can take responsibility without taking blame for your worth. You can name mistakes without turning them into character flaws. You can see patterns without condemning yourself for having them. Clarity without shame is the discipline of separating **behavior from identity**. You are responsible for your actions. You are not reducible to them.

Learning to Look Without Collapsing

One of the most important rebuilding skills is learning to observe your life without emotionally imploding. Your nervous system cannot tell the difference between truth and threat until you teach it. This means learning to say things like:

- "This choice didn't work."
- "This pattern isn't serving me."
- "This situation requires change."

Without adding:

- "…because I'm weak."
- "…because I always fail."
- "…because I can't be trusted."

Clarity is descriptive, not evaluative. It names what *is*, not what you *are*. When rebuilders learn this distinction, something powerful happens:

- They stop defending themselves against reality.
- They stop arguing with facts.
- They stop rewriting history to protect their ego.
- They stop collapsing under the information they need to move forward.

A New Way to Practice Honesty

Clarity without shame is a practice, not a personality trait. It begins with asking better questions.

Not: *"Why am I like this?"* But: **"What is happening here?"**

Not: *"How did I mess this up again?"* But: **"What choice led to this outcome?"**

Not: *"What's wrong with me?"* But: **"What needs attention?"**

This shift turns honesty into a tool instead of a weapon.

Practice: The Neutral Inventory

Set aside 20 minutes. Write without commentary, judgment, or explanation. Divide a page into three sections:

1. What is working right now

List only facts. No minimizing. No qualifying.

2. What is not working right now

Again, facts only. No emotional language. No conclusions.

3. What feels unclear or unstable

Name areas of confusion without forcing answers.

When you're done, read it back once. Do not correct it. Do not justify it. Do not attack yourself for it. This exercise trains your nervous system to tolerate truth without collapse.

Why This Matters Before Moving Forward

    A. You cannot build a strategy on distortion.

    B. You cannot build a structure on denial.

    C. You cannot build stability on stories designed to protect you from discomfort.

Clarity without shame gives you solid ground.

It allows you to say: *"This is where I am."* Without saying: *"And that means I'm unworthy."*

That distinction is everything. Because the rebuild ahead will ask you to make decisions, set boundaries, choose paths, and release others. None of that is possible if every moment of clarity triggers self-punishment. Truth is not the enemy... Shame is.

When truth is met with steadiness instead of self-attack, it becomes liberating. It becomes usable. It becomes the foundation for real change. In the next chapter, we'll build on this clarity by learning how to see patterns, not as proof of failure, but as information that guides the rebuild forward.

CHAPTER 13

Grounded Decision-Making

Integrating wisdom, self-awareness, and lived experience.

Rebuilding requires decisions. Small ones. Hard ones. Quiet ones no one applauds. And visible ones that feel heavy with consequence.

After a collapse, decision-making often becomes distorted. People hesitate, rush, avoid, or overthink. Not because they lack intelligence or discipline, but because collapse destabilizes the internal systems that once guided choice. After a collapse, your nervous system often reacts faster than your reasoning. This chapter is not about making *perfect* decisions. It's about making *grounded* ones.

Grounded decision-making is the ability to choose from clarity rather than fear, identity rather than urgency, and truth rather than survival instinct. It is the bridge between inner restoration and external rebuilding.

Why Decision-Making Breaks After Collapse

Collapse disrupts trust, especially self-trust. You stop trusting your judgment because:

- Past decisions led to pain

- Outcomes felt unpredictable
- External pressure replaced internal guidance
- Fear became louder than intuition
- Shame questioned your competence

So you either:

- Delay decisions indefinitely
- Outsource decisions to others
- Over-research to avoid responsibility
- React emotionally
- Or choose speed to escape discomfort

None of these create stability. Rebuilding requires a new decision framework, one that doesn't rely on adrenaline, ego, or perfection.

The Common Thread Across Every Wise System

Across Stoicism, Human Design, CBT, and lived experience, one truth repeats: **Good decisions come from self-regulation, not urgency.** Different traditions say it differently, but they all point to the same foundation:

- Calm before choice
- Awareness before action
- Alignment before execution

This chapter gives you a simple, human way to apply that wisdom without needing to "believe" in any one system.

The Stoic Contribution: Control What Is Yours

Stoicism teaches a powerful distinction: Some things are within your control. Some things are not. Collapse often blurs this line. You try to control outcomes, people, systems, timing, and perception, while neglecting the one thing that *is* always yours: your response.

Grounded decisions begin with this question: **What part of this situation is actually mine to choose?**

- Not the result.
- Not the reaction of others.
- Not the timeline.

But:

- Your behavior
- Your values
- Your boundaries
- Your next step

When rebuilders anchor decisions here, anxiety decreases and clarity increases. Stoicism doesn't ask you to feel less; it asks you to choose from what is yours.

The CBT Contribution: Thoughts Shape Choices

Cognitive Behavioral Therapy reminds us that decisions are not driven by reality alone, but by interpretation. After collapse, common thinking errors appear:

"If I choose wrong, everything will fall apart."

"I don't get second chances."

"This decision defines me." // *"I can't afford another mistake."*

These thoughts feel true, but they are not facts. These distortions aren't flaws; they're protective patterns. Grounded decision-making requires examining the thought before obeying it.

Ask:

- Is this fear-based or fact-based?
- Is this about now, or about the past repeating itself?
- Is this decision actually irreversible?

Most decisions are not life sentences. They are course corrections.

The Human Design Contribution: Honoring Your Decision Style

One of the most overlooked causes of bad decisions is using someone else's decision-making style.

- Some people need time.
- Some need to talk it out.
- Some need emotional clarity first.
- Some need data.
- Some need quiet.

Collapse often forces people into urgency, overriding their natural process. Grounded decision-making requires honoring *how* you decide best, not how you think you should. The right decision made the wrong way still destabilizes you. Your timing is part of your decision style.

Lived Experience: Decisions Improve With Integrity, Not Confidence

Confidence is often misframed as certainty. But in rebuilding, certainty is rare. What matters more is integrity. Integrity means:

- You chose from alignment
- You respected your limits
- You didn't abandon yourself
- You accepted uncertainty without panic

Many of the strongest decisions are quiet. They don't feel heroic. They feel steady. And that steadiness compounds.

The Grounded Decision Framework

Before making an important decision, walk through these five steps:

Step 1. Regulate first

If you are emotionally charged, you are not deciding; you are reacting. Pause. Breathe. Stabilize.

Step 2. Separate facts from fears

List what you know versus what you assume.

Step 3. Identify what is actually yours to control

Focus on action, not outcome.

Step 4. Check alignment

Ask:

- Does this move me toward stability?
- Does this honor my dignity?
- Does this fit the person I am becoming?

Step 5. Choose the next right step, not the perfect one

Rebuilding happens through direction, not certainty.

Practice: The Grounded Choice Pause

When facing a decision, write these sentences:

- "The decision I'm facing is ___."
- "What I'm afraid will happen is ___."
- "What I know for certain is ___."
- "What I can control is ___."
- "The next grounded step is ___."

Then act. This practice retrains trust in yourself.

Why This Chapter Matters Now

You are entering the phase of rebuilding where clarity turns into motion. Decisions will shape your days, your structure, your work, and your future stability. Grounded decision-making ensures that motion does not recreate the chaos you just survived. This is not about being fearless. It's about being steady.

In the next chapter, we will move from individual decisions into pattern recognition, learning how to see your life clearly over time, not as isolated moments, but as signals guiding the rebuild forward.

Pillar 3:
Tools & Skill Building

CHAPTER 14

Capability Over Complexity

Why rebuilders need simple, actionable tools,
not jargon or overwhelm.

R ebuilding does not fail because people lack intelligence. It fails
because they are given systems they cannot carry. After a collapse,
many rebuilders are handed complexity disguised as help. Complexity
increases cognitive load, and cognitive load increases collapse.
Complexity brings:

- Dense frameworks
- Endless acronyms
- Overengineered plans
- Advice that assumes energy they do not have

The result is predictable. They feel behind before they begin.
Ashamed for not keeping up. Overwhelmed instead of equipped.
This chapter establishes a core truth of Built for Rebuilding:

Capability comes before sophistication.

If a tool cannot be used in real life, under real stress, by a real
person rebuilding from real collapse, it is not a tool. It is noise.

Why Complexity Feels Like Progress (But Isn't)

Complexity often masquerades as competence. It looks impressive. It sounds intelligent. It creates the illusion of mastery. But complexity is rarely designed for the person who is rebuilding. It is designed for the person who is already stable. Rebuilders need tools that:

- Reduce cognitive load
- Work under emotional stress
- Fit inside unpredictable days
- Build confidence through use, not explanation

Complexity delays action. Capability enables it.

The Rebuilder's Reality

People rebuilding their lives are not starting from neutral. They are often navigating:

- Emotional exhaustion
- Financial pressure
- Identity instability
- Decision fatigue
- Limited time and energy
- Fear of getting it wrong again

In that state, asking someone to "optimize," "scale," or "strategize" without first restoring basic capability is irresponsible. Before people can build systems, they must rebuild skills.

The Difference Between Knowing and Being Able

One of the most damaging myths in self-help and business culture is this: "If you understand it, you can do it." That is not true during a rebuild. Knowing does not equal capability. Insight does not equal execution. Awareness does not equal skill. When people confuse knowing with being able, they blame themselves instead of the tool. Capability is built through:

- Repetition
- Simplicity
- Feedback
- Safe practice
- Real-world application

This book is not interested in what you *know*. It is interested in what you can *do* when it matters.

What "Tools" Actually Mean in a Rebuild

In Built for Rebuilding, tools are not abstract ideas. They are:

- Decision frameworks you can use under pressure
- Communication tools that reduce conflict
- Financial basics that restore stability
- Time and energy tools that prevent burnout
- Emotional tools that prevent collapse
- Systems that work even on hard days

A good tool does three things:

1. It lowers friction
2. It increases consistency
3. It restores agency

If it does not do all three, it is not ready for a rebuilder.

Why Simple Tools Are Not "Basic"

There is a misunderstanding that simple tools are elementary or unsophisticated. In reality, simplicity is refinement. A tool that works

111

reliably, under stress, with limited energy, is far more advanced than a system that only works when conditions are perfect. Simplicity is what remains after everything unnecessary has been removed. Rebuilders do not need brilliance. They need reliability. When people think knowing is the same as 'able to do', they take the blame, not the tool. They need tools that:

- Can be explained in minutes
- Can be used without motivation
- Can be repeated without burnout
- Can be trusted when clarity wavers

Simple tools build momentum. Momentum builds belief. Belief rebuilds identity.

Capability Is the Antidote to Shame

When people cannot execute what they are taught, they assume something is wrong with them.

"I should be able to do this."

"Everyone else seems to get it."

"I must be failing again."

This is not a motivation problem. It is a tool design problem. Capability restores dignity because it produces evidence. Each small success says:

"I can do this."

"I can follow through."

"I can build from here."

That evidence matters more than inspiration.

The Built for Rebuilding Tool Standard

Every tool introduced in this book will meet these standards:

- It can be used immediately
- It requires no special background
- It works under imperfect conditions
- It builds confidence through action
- It prioritizes stability over speed

We are not trying to impress you. We are trying to equip you.

Practice: The Tool Filter

Before adopting any tool, system, or advice, ask:

- Can I use this on my hardest day?
- Does this reduce or increase overwhelm?
- Does this require me to be someone I'm not yet?
- Will this build confidence through use?
- Does this fit the life I'm rebuilding into?

If the answer is no, set it aside. A good tool doesn't require you to become someone else to use it. Rebuilding is not the time to collect tools. It is the time to choose the right ones.

Why This Chapter Comes Before Skill Building

Before we teach skills, we must establish the rules. You are not here to master everything. You are here to rebuild steadily. You do not need more information. You need fewer tools that actually work. In the chapters that follow, we will introduce practical skills in:

- Decision-making
- Time and energy management
- Financial stability
- Communication
- Work and life structure

Each one is designed to build real capability, not theoretical competence. Because rebuilding succeeds not when life becomes complex again, but when you become capable of handling it. And that is where true strength is rebuilt.

CHAPTER 15

Emotional and Mental Tools for Rebuilders

Self-regulation, confidence rebuilding,
resilience without toxicity

R ebuilding is not only practical work. It is emotional work. Your
nervous system reacts before your reasoning does; tools help you
close that gap. And for many people, this is where rebuilding quietly
fails. Not because they lack strength. Not because they lack willpower.
But because no one ever taught them how to regulate themselves once
the old structures fell away.

After a collapse, emotions are louder. Thoughts feel heavier.
Confidence feels fragile. Pressure feels constant. If rebuilders are
given a strategy without emotional tools, they will eventually burn
out, sabotage progress, or retreat back into survival.

This chapter introduces the emotional and mental tools that allow
rebuilders to stay steady without hardening, resilient without becoming
toxic, and confident without pretending.

Why Emotional Tools Matter More After Collapse

Before collapse, many people functioned by override:

- Push harder
- Ignore discomfort
- Stay busy
- Perform through stress
- Power through emotion

Collapse removes the ability to override. The nervous system is already taxed. The mind is already vigilant. The emotional margin is thinner. Without tools, people react instead of respond. They spiral instead of stabilize. They confuse discomfort with danger. Emotional tools are not about avoiding feeling. They are about staying present without being overwhelmed.

Self-Regulation: The Foundation of Emotional Stability

Self-regulation is the ability to stay in control of your behavior even when your emotions are activated. It does not mean calm all the time… It means **capacity**.

Collapse often leaves people in one of two states:

- Hyper-reactive, everything feels urgent
- Numb, disconnected, and withdrawn

Both states sabotage rebuilding. Self-regulation restores the space between stimulus and response.

Tool 1: The Pause Practice

Before reacting, pause long enough to interrupt the automatic response. Ask yourself:

- "What am I feeling right now?"

- "What does this feeling want me to do?"
- "What response would actually help?"

You are not suppressing emotion. You are choosing your response. That choice is power returning.

Tool 2: Body-Based Grounding

Rebuilders often try to think their way out of emotional overload. But regulation starts in the body. Simple grounding actions:

- Slow breathing
- Feet flat on the floor
- Shoulders relaxed
- Longer exhales than inhales

When the body settles, the mind follows. Stability begins physically before it becomes cognitive.

Confidence Rebuilding Without Performance

After collapse, confidence rarely disappears overnight. It erodes through:

- Repeated loss
- Broken trust in self
- Decisions that backfired
- Shame layered over failure

Traditional confidence advice fails rebuilders because it demands belief before evidence. Rebuilders need the opposite.

Confidence is rebuilt through proof, not affirmation.

Tool 3: Evidence Over Emotion

Confidence grows when you give yourself evidence you can trust. Each completed action becomes proof:

- "I followed through."
- "I handled that."
- "I didn't quit."
- "I made a grounded choice."

Confidence does not require optimism. It requires consistency.

Tool 4: The Evidence Journal

Each day, write one sentence:

"Today I proved to myself that I can ___."

Examples:

- "…stay calm under pressure."
- "…finish something small."
- "…tell the truth."
- "…take care of myself."
- "…keep going."

Small evidence accumulates. Belief follows behavior.

Resilience Without Toxicity

Resilience is often misunderstood. In many cultures, resilience has been weaponized:

- "Just toughen up."
- "Push through."
- "Don't feel it."
- "Be grateful it wasn't worse."

This version of resilience breaks people. Healthy resilience is not endurance without rest. It is recovery with intention. Resilience is not measured by how much you endure, but by how well you recover. True resilience includes:

- Boundaries

- Rest
- Emotional honesty
- Self-compassion
- Sustainability

Rebuilders do not need to be harder. They need to be steadier.

Tool 5: The Sustainable Pace Rule

Ask yourself regularly:

- "Can I maintain this pace for six months?"
- "What would make this sustainable instead of impressive?"
- "What am I forcing instead of building?"

Burnout is not a badge of honor. It is a warning signal. Resilience grows when effort matches capacity.

Thought Tools for Emotional Stability

Collapse distorts thinking. Common patterns include:

- Catastrophizing
- All-or-nothing thinking
- Personalization
- Hopeless forecasting
- Self-attack disguised as accountability

These thoughts feel true, but they are not accurate.

Tool 6: Thought Clarification

When a distressing thought appears, ask:

- "Is this a fact or an interpretation?"
- "What evidence actually supports this?"
- "What would I tell someone I care about?"

Thought clarity is not positive thinking. It is accurate thinking. Accurate thinking requires compassion, not criticism. Accuracy restores calm.

Emotional Strength Is Learned, Not Inherited

Many rebuilders believe emotional steadiness is a personality trait… It is not. It is a skill set. No one taught most people how to:

- Regulate emotion
- Recover after stress
- Build confidence safely
- Stay grounded during uncertainty

This chapter exists because those skills can be learned.

Practice: Your Emotional Tool Kit

Choose three tools from this chapter to practice daily for the next two weeks:

- One body-based tool
- One confidence-building tool
- One thought clarification tool

Do not try to master everything. Build familiarity first. Familiarity creates safety. Safety creates capacity.

Why These Tools Come Before External Skills

Emotional tools protect the rebuild.

- They prevent self-sabotage.
- They reduce burnout.
- They stabilize decision-making.
- They keep progress intact when life pushes back.

You do not need to eliminate emotion to rebuild. You need to learn how to carry it. That is emotional strength. And it is one of the most important capabilities you will rebuild. Confidence is not who you are… It's what you practice.

CHAPTER 16

Practical Tools for Life, Work, and Business

*Communication, planning, financial basics,
entrepreneurship foundations*

R ebuilding does not happen in theory. It happens in conversations, calendars, bank accounts, and daily decisions. This chapter focuses on practical tools, not because they are glamorous, but because they are stabilizing. When life collapses, the basics are often the first things to break:

- Communication becomes reactive or avoidant
- Planning feels overwhelming or pointless
- Money becomes a source of fear instead of clarity
- Work loses structure or meaning

Rebuilders don't need perfection in these areas. They need **function**. The tools in this chapter are designed to restore basic operating capacity in life, work, and business, so rebuilding becomes livable instead of exhausting.

Communication Tools: Speaking Clearly Without Defensiveness

Collapse changes how people communicate.

- Some withdraw.
- Some overexplain.
- Some become guarded.
- Some react emotionally.
- Some avoid hard conversations entirely.

Clear communication is not about being polished. It is about being grounded.

The Rebuilder's Communication Rule

Say what is true, without attack or apology.

- Not everything needs justification.
- Not every boundary needs explanation.
- Not every feeling needs defense.

Tool: The Three-Part Communication Frame

When something matters, speak in this order:

1. **Observation**

   "Here's what I'm seeing or experiencing."

2. **Impact**

   "Here's how it's affecting me."

3. **Request or Boundary**

   "Here's what I need or what I'm choosing."

Example:

"I've noticed our meetings keep running over time. It's affecting my focus and energy. I need to keep our meetings to the scheduled window."

This frame reduces conflict because it removes accusation and centers clarity.

Planning Tools: From Overwhelm to Order

After collapse, planning often feels unsafe. People think:

- "What's the point?"
- "Everything changes anyway."
- "I'll plan when I feel stable."

But stability comes *from* planning, not before it.

The Rebuilder's Planning Principle

Plan small. Plan honestly. Plan for reality, not optimism.

Tool: The Three-Horizon Planner

Instead of long-range pressure, use three short horizons:

- **Today**: What must be done today?
- **This Week**: What matters this week?
- **This Month**: What would help this month?

That's it.

No five-year plans.

No fantasy calendars.

No pressure to optimize.

Clarity grows when plans are survivable.

Financial Basics: Removing Fear Through Visibility

Money becomes emotionally charged after a collapse. People:

- Avoid looking.
- Avoid budgeting.
- Avoid conversations.
- Avoid decisions.

Avoidance creates anxiety. Visibility creates control. You do not need advanced financial strategy to rebuild. You need basic awareness.

Tool: The Financial Grounding Snapshot

Once per week, write down:

- Current cash available
- Known expenses coming up
- One financial priority for the week

No judgment. No shame. No analysis... Just truth. Stability begins when money stops being a mystery.

Work Tools: Creating Structure Where None Exists

Many rebuilders experience work instability:

- Job loss
- Career shifts
- Consulting or gig work
- Entrepreneurship at zero
- Reentry barriers

Without structure, work becomes chaotic and draining.

Tool: The Workday Anchor

Every workday should include:

- One start ritual
- One focused work block
- One clear stopping point

Rituals create psychological safety. Safety supports consistency. Work becomes sustainable when it has edges.

Entrepreneurship Foundations
(For Those Building Something New)

Entrepreneurship attracts rebuilders because it promises control and possibility. But without foundation, it recreates chaos. Entrepreneurship is not an escape from rebuilding. It is a **discipline within it**.

The Rebuilder's Entrepreneur Rule

Build slowly enough to stay intact. Before scaling, focus on:

- Who you serve
- What problem you solve
- How you create value
- How you sustain yourself while doing it

Tool: The One-Sentence Clarity Test

Complete this sentence: "I help ___ solve ___ by ___." If you can't explain it simply, it's not ready. Clarity precedes growth.

Integration: Life, Work, and Business Are Not Separate

One of the biggest mistakes rebuilders make is compartmentalizing:

- "This is my personal life."
- "This is my work life."
- "This is my rebuilding life."

They are the same life. The tools you use to:

- Communicate clearly
- Plan realistically
- Handle money honestly
- Structure your days
- Build capability

…are the same tools that create stability everywhere.

Practice: The Weekly Rebuild Check-In

Once per week, answer these questions:

- Where did communication feel clear?
- Where did planning reduce stress?
- What did I learn about my finances?
- What worked in my daily structure?
- What needs to simplify next week?

This is not evaluation. It is calibration.

Why These Tools Matter

These tools do not make life perfect. They make it workable. Rebuilding succeeds not because everything improves at once, but because fewer things are on fire at the same time. Practical tools:

- Reduce friction
- Restore confidence
- Protect energy
- Create forward motion

They give rebuilders something they desperately need: A life that holds together while they build the next chapter. With capability restored, we now move into **Pillar 4: Structure & Strategy**, where effort becomes organized, direction becomes clear, and rebuilding turns into something you can sustain.

The rebuild is no longer fragile. It is taking shape.

Pillar 4:
Structure & Strategy

CHAPTER 17

Chaos Isn't a Strategy

Why most rebuilds fail: no structure, no sequencing, no plan

Most rebuilds don't fail because people quit. They fail because every-thing is happening at once. After a collapse, people are told to:

- Heal
- Hustle
- Plan
- Pivot
- Grow
- Reinvent
- Be patient
- Move fast

All at the same time. The result isn't progress. It's chaos dressed up as effort. This chapter introduces a hard truth that rebuilders often resist at first: **Intensity is not strategy. Movement is not direction. Chaos is not growth.** Rebuilding requires structure, not urgency.

Why Chaos Feels Like Momentum

When life falls apart, doing *something* feels better than doing nothing. Chaos provides:

- A sense of motion
- Temporary relief from fear
- Distraction from uncertainty
- The illusion of control

But chaos has no memory. No sequencing. No protection. You expend energy without building anything that lasts. Rebuilders often mistake activity for progress because progress feels slow at first.

The Cost of Unstructured Rebuilding

When there is no structure:

- Decisions are reactive
- Energy is scattered
- Confidence erodes
- Burnout accelerates
- Wins don't compound
- Nothing stabilizes

People bounce between:

- Emotional work and avoidance
- Big plans and paralysis
- Hope and exhaustion
- Effort and collapse

This is not a motivation problem. It is a structural one.

Structure Is Not Restriction

Many rebuilders resist structure because it feels limiting. They think:

- "I don't want to box myself in."
- "I need flexibility."
- "I'll structure things once I feel better."

But structure is not a cage. It is a container. Structure protects:

- Energy
- Focus
- Emotional stability
- Decision-making
- Momentum

Without structure, life decides for you.

Why Sequencing Matters More Than Speed

Rebuilding is not about doing everything. It's about doing the *right* things in the *right* order. When sequencing is ignored:

- People chase income before identity
- Strategy before clarity
- Growth before stability
- Pressure before capacity

This creates fragile success. Sequencing respects reality. You don't build a roof before a foundation. You don't scale before you stabilize. You don't optimize what hasn't been established.

The Rebuilder's Rule of Order

Every rebuild must move through these stages, whether acknowledged or not:

1. **Stabilize**

   Reduce chaos. Create safety. Restore basic function.

2. **Clarify**

   Understand where you are and what matters now.

3. **Build Capability**

   Develop skills and confidence through repetition.

4. **Create Structure**

   Organize effort so it compounds.

5. **Apply Strategy**

   Direct energy toward intentional outcomes.

Skipping steps doesn't save time. It creates setbacks.

Structure Reduces Emotional Load

One of the hidden benefits of structure is emotional relief. When you know:

- What happens today
- What doesn't happen yet
- What matters now
- What can wait

…your nervous system settles. Structure answers the question: "What am I responsible for right now?" And that clarity prevents overwhelm.

Chaos Keeps You Stuck in Reaction

Chaos forces constant decision-making. Every moment becomes:

- "What should I do next?"
- "Am I doing enough?"
- "Is this right?"
- "Should I change direction?"

This drains energy and confidence. Structure removes unnecessary decisions. When decisions are fewer, choices are better.

Practice: The Chaos Audit

Write down everything you're currently trying to rebuild:

- Personal
- Financial

- Career
- Health
- Relationships
- Identity
- Stability

Now ask:

- Which of these must be addressed *now*?
- Which of these can wait?
- Which of these is adding chaos instead of stability?

Circle the top **three**. Everything else is not failure. It is sequencing.

Why This Chapter Matters Now

1. You've rebuilt dignity.
2. You've restored agency.
3. You've developed tools.

Now it's time to **organize effort**. Structure is the bridge between intention and outcome. Without it, even the strongest rebuild collapses under its own weight. In the next chapters, we'll define:

- What structure actually looks like
- How to create sequencing without rigidity
- How to design systems that protect your rebuild instead of draining it

Because rebuilding succeeds not when life becomes busy again, but when it becomes **organized enough to hold what you're building**. Chaos isn't a strategy. Structure is.

CHAPTER 18

The Rebuilder's Pathway

Introducing The Rebuilder's Pathway

R ebuilding does not happen in a straight line, but it does follow a pattern. Every lasting rebuild I've witnessed, including my own, moves through the same sequence. When people struggle, it's rarely because they aren't trying hard enough. It's because they are working out of order. This chapter introduces the **Rebuilder's Pathway**, the structural backbone that holds everything in Built for Rebuilding together:

- Identity
- Clarity
- Strategy
- Tactics
- Stability

This is not a productivity model. It's not a hustle framework. It's an order of operations for rebuilding a life that doesn't collapse under pressure.

Why Order Matters More Than Effort

Most rebuilders work backward. They start with tactics:

137

- Apply for jobs
- Launch something new
- Make more money
- Fix the surface problems

When that doesn't work, they jump to strategy:

- New plans
- New directions
- New ideas

But without clarity, strategy becomes guessing. Without identity, clarity collapses under pressure. Effort applied out of sequence creates frustration, not progress. The pathway exists to prevent that.

Stage 1: Identity

Who you are now, not who you were? Identity is always first, whether you acknowledge it or not. Collapse fractures identity:

- Confidence erodes
- Direction disappears
- Self-trust weakens
- Worth feels conditional

If identity is unstable, everything built on top of it is fragile. This is why Parts II and III of this book focus so heavily on dignity, agency, and self-belief. Before you decide what to do next, you must stabilize who you are becoming.

Identity answers:

- Who am I now?
- What matters to me?
- What am I no longer willing to sacrifice?
- What kind of life am I rebuilding toward?

Without these answers, progress doesn't stick.

Stage 2: Clarity

Seeing reality without distortion. Clarity is the ability to see your life honestly, without shame or fantasy. This includes:

- Your current constraints
- Your actual capacity
- Your responsibilities
- Your resources
- Your limitations
- Your opportunities

Clarity replaces confusion with orientation. It answers:

- Where am I right now?
- What's real?
- What's within my control?
- What matters most in this season?

Clarity doesn't make decisions for you. It makes good decisions possible.

Stage 3: Strategy

Choosing direction, not doing everything. Strategy is where many rebuilders rush too early. But strategy without identity and clarity is pressure, not guidance. Real strategy answers:

- What am I building *now*?
- What am I not building yet?
- What deserves my energy?
- What can wait?

Strategy is about direction, not volume. It limits choices so effort can compound instead of scatter.

Stage 4: Tactics

Turning intention into action. Tactics are the daily actions that bring strategy to life. This is where:
- Plans become steps
- Ideas become behavior
- Consistency replaces intensity

Tactics are only effective when they serve strategy. Without that connection, tactics become busywork. Tactics answer:
- What do I do today?
- What do I do this week?
- What is the next right step?

Good tactics are boring, repeatable, and sustainable.

Stage 5: Stability

When the rebuild begins to hold. Stability is not perfection. It is durability. Stability shows up as:
- Predictable routines
- Reliable income or progress toward it
- Emotional steadiness
- Fewer crises
- Clear boundaries
- Forward momentum

Stability is not the end of growth. It is the platform that allows growth without collapse. When stability arrives, rebuilding shifts from survival to stewardship.

Why People Get Stuck

Most rebuilders get stuck because they:
- Try to create stability through tactics alone

- Chase strategy without clarity
- Avoid identity work because it feels uncomfortable
- Rush sequencing out of fear

The pathway removes guesswork. When you're stuck, ask:

- Which stage am I actually in?
- Which stage am I trying to skip?

Progress resumes when order is restored.

Practice: Locate Yourself on the Pathway

Right now, ask yourself:

- Which stage am I truly in?
- What stage am I trying to force?
- What would it look like to work where I am, not where I wish I were?

There is no penalty for being early in the pathway. There is only risk in pretending you're further along.

The Pathway Is Not Linear, But It Is Directional

You may revisit stages. Life will test stability. New identity questions will surface. Clarity will need refreshing. That's all normal. What matters is knowing the order and respecting it.

The rebuild doesn't succeed because you moved fast. It succeeds because you moved **in sequence**. In the next chapter, we'll move deeper into how to build structure around this pathway so effort compounds, energy is protected, and rebuilding becomes sustainable instead of exhausting.

The rebuild now has a map: **Identity | Clarity | Strategy | Tactics | Stability.** And maps change everything.

CHAPTER 19

Building a Life
You Can Actually Sustain

Systems, routines, structure,
and the daily grind done with intention

Most rebuilds don't fail because people stop trying. They fail because the rebuild asks them to live in a way they cannot maintain.

- Unsustainable routines.
- Unrealistic expectations.
- Overloaded days.
- Constant urgency.
- No margin for life.

At first, adrenaline carries the effort. Then reality arrives.

This chapter is about designing a rebuild that fits inside a real human life. Not the ideal version of you. Not the motivated version of you. Not the version of you on your best day. The version of you who wakes up tired, gets interrupted, has responsibilities, and still wants to keep moving forward. Sustainability is not a luxury in rebuilding… It is the requirement.

Why Sustainability Is the Real Measure of Success

In a rebuild, progress that cannot be repeated is not progress.

- Anyone can sprint for a few weeks.
- Anyone can overhaul everything at once.
- Anyone can push through temporarily.

But rebuilding is not a short season. It is a transition into a new normal. If your systems require:

- Constant motivation
- High emotional output
- Perfect discipline
- Unlimited time
- Unlimited energy

They will eventually collapse. Sustainability answers one question: *Can I live this way without breaking myself again?*

The Daily Grind Is Where Rebuilds Are Won or Lost

Most rebuilding happens in ordinary moments:

- Mornings
- Workdays
- Evenings
- Weekends
- Repeated decisions
- Small habits

There is no dramatic montage. No single breakthrough. No final arrival. The daily grind is not the enemy. It is the environment. When the grind is chaotic, rebuilding is fragile. When the grind is intentional, rebuilding becomes durable.

Systems Before Motivation

Motivation fluctuates. Systems remain. A system is simply a repeatable way of doing something that reduces decision-making and emotional load. Good systems:

- Remove friction
- Protect energy
- Create predictability
- Support consistency

Rebuilders don't need more motivation. They need fewer decisions.

Designing Systems That Work on Hard Days

Every system you build should pass this test: **Can I follow this on a bad day?**

If the answer is no, it's too complex. Start with systems for:

- Mornings
- Work blocks
- Meals
- Money check-ins
- Evenings
- Weekly resets

Simple beats perfect. Consistency beats intensity.

Routines as Emotional Safety

Routines are not boring. They are stabilizing. After a collapse, the nervous system craves predictability. A routine says:

"This part of my life is handled."

"I know what happens next."

"I don't have to decide everything."

Routines restore trust between you and your life. They reduce anxiety not by fixing everything, but by removing uncertainty.

The Minimum Effective Day

One of the most important concepts in sustainable rebuilding is this: **Define your minimum effective day.** This is the smallest version of a "good enough" day that still moves the rebuild forward. Your minimum day might include:

- One focused task
- One grounding practice
- One honest conversation
- One act of self-care
- One financial or planning check-in

On strong days, you'll do more. On hard days, you do the minimum. The minimum keeps the rebuild alive.

Structure Without Rigidity

Structure does not mean over-scheduling. It means:

- Clear start times
- Clear stop times
- Clear priorities
- Clear rest

A sustainable structure includes:

- White space
- Recovery time
- Flexibility for life
- Permission to pause

Rebuilders do not need tighter control. They need smarter boundaries.

The Role of Rest in Sustainability

Rest is not a reward for progress. It is a requirement for it. Without rest:

- Decision quality declines
- Emotions spike
- Motivation collapses
- Old patterns return

Rest is not quitting. It is maintenance. A rebuild without rest is a rebuild on borrowed time.

Practice: The Sustainability Check

Once a week, ask yourself:

- What drained me this week?
- What restored me?
- What felt sustainable?
- What felt forced?
- What needs simplifying next week?

Then adjust. Rebuilding is iterative, not fixed.

Why This Chapter Matters Now

You now have:

- Identity
- Clarity
- Tools
- Structure
- Strategy

This chapter ensures those things can live together without collapsing under their own weight. A sustainable life is not smaller. It is steadier. And steadiness is what allows rebuilding to last. In the next chapter, we'll complete **Pillar 4** by looking at how strategy evolves over time, how to adapt without destabilizing, and how to keep the rebuild aligned as life changes.

Because the goal is not just to rebuild... It's to stay rebuilt.

Pillar 5:
Income & Stability

CHAPTER 20

Stability Is Not Optional

Why rebuilding collapses
without a foundation of income and structure

T here is a version of rebuilding that sounds noble, spiritual, and
incomplete. It says:

"Focus on healing first."

"Money will come later."

"Don't worry about income yet."

"Just find yourself."

That version of rebuilding collapses quietly, and often painfully.
Because the truth is simple: **You cannot rebuild a life on instability.**

- You can grow insight without income.
- You can heal without structure.
- You can clarify identity without financial grounding.

But you cannot *sustain* a rebuild without stability. This chapter
names something many rebuilding narratives avoid saying out loud:
**Stability is not a reward for rebuilding. It is the condition that
makes rebuilding possible.**

Why Stability Is Often Avoided in Rebuild Conversations

Stability is uncomfortable to talk about because it forces realism. It asks questions like:

- How will I support myself?
- What will keep a roof over my head?
- What happens if this takes longer than expected?
- What pressure am I carrying every day because income is uncertain?

Many rebuilders avoid these questions because they feel overwhelming, shame-inducing, or limiting. Others avoid them because they associate income with:

- Past burnout
- Toxic work culture
- Capitalist pressure
- Identity wounds
- Systems that failed them

But avoiding stability doesn't make those wounds heal. It makes them louder.

Stability Is Not About Wealth

It's About Grounding. This chapter is not about getting rich. It is not about hustle. It is not about status or performance. Stability means:

- Predictable income or progress toward it
- Manageable expenses
- Reduced financial panic
- The ability to plan beyond tomorrow
- Enough margin to make grounded decisions

Stability creates breathing room. Without breathing room, every decision feels urgent. Urgency destroys clarity. And clarity is the backbone of rebuilding.

The Nervous System and Income Are Connected

This is not philosophical. It is biological. When income is unstable:

- The nervous system stays activated
- Stress becomes chronic
- Decision-making degrades
- Risk tolerance collapses or spikes irrationally
- Old survival patterns return

People don't make long-term decisions when they're afraid of short-term survival. Income stability calms the system enough for rebuilding to hold.

Why Identity Work Alone Is Not Enough

Earlier in this book, we centered dignity and identity for a reason. But identity without income becomes fragile.

- You can believe you're worthy.
- You can reclaim agency.
- You can design a new self.

But if you are constantly worried about rent, food, transportation, or basic security, that identity is under siege. This is why Built for Rebuilding does not separate:

- Personal growth
- Structural support
- Economic reality

They are not different journeys. They are one system.

Stability Before Optimization

Many rebuilders fall into one of two traps:

Trap One: Waiting for the "right" opportunity… They delay income while searching for alignment, purpose, or the perfect next step.

Trap Two: Overreaching too early… They chase high-risk opportunities hoping to skip the hard middle.

Both traps destabilize the rebuild. Stability comes first. Optimization comes later. A stable rebuild does not ask: *"How do I maximize income right now?"* It asks: *"How do I make this livable while I rebuild?"*

What Stability Actually Requires

Stability is built from a few foundational elements:

- **A reliable income source**, even if it's temporary
- **Clear financial visibility**, not avoidance
- **A basic budget**, not perfection
- **Work that does not drain all capacity**
- **A plan that matches current energy, not past ambition**

This may not look impressive. It may not feel like **"progress."** But it is the scaffolding that keeps the rebuild standing.

Income Is a Tool, Not an Identity

One of the most damaging beliefs rebuilders carry is this: *"My income defines my worth."* That belief must be dismantled. But dismantling it does not require rejecting income. It requires reframing it.

- Income is not identity.
- Income is **infrastructure.**

It supports:

- Housing
- Food

- Healthcare
- Transportation
- Time
- Choice

When income is treated as infrastructure, it loses its emotional charge. It becomes a support beam, not a verdict.

Practice: The Stability Reality Check

Answer these questions honestly, without judgment:

- What income do I currently rely on?
- How predictable is it?
- What are my non-negotiable expenses?
- Where am I experiencing the most financial pressure?
- What would "enough for now" actually look like?

You are not committing to this forever. You are committing to stability *for this season*.

Why This Chapter Matters Right Now

- You've rebuilt the self.
- You've created clarity.
- You've learned tools.
- You've designed structure.
- You've built a sustainable rhythm.

Now comes the foundation that allows all of that to continue.

Stability does not limit rebuilding. It protects it.

Without stability:

- Progress fractures
- Anxiety resurges

- Identity erodes
- Strategy collapses
- Hope becomes exhausting

With stability:

- Decisions improve
- Energy returns
- Planning becomes possible
- Growth becomes intentional

Rebuilding does not mean choosing between meaning and money. It means building a life where meaning can exist *because* stability is present. In the next chapter, we'll talk about **practical pathways to income during a rebuild**, how to choose work that supports recovery rather than undermines it, and how to build toward long-term stability without recreating the patterns that caused collapse in the first place.

Stability is not optional… It is the ground beneath your feet.

CHAPTER 21

Employment, Entrepreneurship, or Both?

The practical pathways to stability
and how to choose your next step

A fter collapse, one of the most pressing questions rebuilders face is deceptively simple: *How am I going to support myself now?* That question often turns into a deeper identity struggle:

- "Am I supposed to go get a job?"
- "Am I meant to build something of my own?"
- "Did entrepreneurship fail me, or did I fail it?"
- "Is going back to work giving up?"
- "Is starting over too risky?"

This chapter exists to remove the pressure, the mythology, and the false binaries around work during a rebuild. Because the truth is this: **There is no single "right" path to stability. There is only the right path for *this season* of your rebuild.**

Why Rebuilders Get Stuck at This Crossroads

Employment and entrepreneurship carry emotional weight. For some:

- Employment feels like safety, structure, and predictability.
- Entrepreneurship feels like freedom, identity, and possibility.

For others:

- Employment feels like confinement or failure.
- Entrepreneurship feels like pressure, risk, and fear.

Rebuilders often make the wrong choice not because they lack insight, but because they confuse *identity* with *infrastructure*. Work is infrastructure. Not a verdict on who you are. Not proof of your worth. Not a permanent decision about your future.

The Core Question Is Not "What Am I Meant to Do?"

The real question is: **What supports stability while I rebuild?** Stability comes first. Identity continues evolving. Purpose clarifies over time. When rebuilders reverse this order, they place unbearable pressure on work to solve everything at once. Work does not need to fulfill you right now. It needs to **support you**.

Path One: Employment as a Stabilizer

Employment is often the fastest path to:

- Predictable income
- Reduced financial anxiety
- Routine and structure
- Time boundaries
- Reduced cognitive load

For many rebuilders, employment is not a step backward. It is a stabilizing platform. Employment works well when:

- You need immediate income
- Your nervous system is still recovering
- You need structure and predictability

- Decision fatigue is high
- Risk tolerance is low

There is dignity in choosing stability. There is wisdom in choosing support. Employment does not erase ambition. It creates breathing room for it.

Path Two: Entrepreneurship as a Builder

Entrepreneurship can be a powerful rebuilding path, but only when entered intentionally. It works best when:

- Basic stability already exists
- Emotional regulation is solid
- Financial pressure is manageable
- Expectations are realistic
- The build is paced, not forced

Entrepreneurship during a rebuild is not about chasing freedom. It is about **designing sustainability**. Rebuilders who succeed in entrepreneurship:

- Start small
- Test ideas
- Build capability gradually
- Separate income needs from identity dreams
- Avoid recreating chaos

Entrepreneurship is not an escape hatch. It is a discipline.

Path Three: The Hybrid Approach

For many rebuilders, the most sustainable option is not either/or. It is **both**. Employment provides:

- Income

- Structure
- Safety

Entrepreneurship provides:
- Optionality
- Growth
- Long-term opportunity

This hybrid approach allows rebuilders to:
- Reduce risk
- Build slowly
- Learn without pressure
- Protect mental health
- Transition intentionally

The hybrid path honors reality without abandoning vision.

Choosing the Right Path for This Season

Ask yourself these questions honestly:
- How stable is my nervous system right now?
- How much financial pressure am I under?
- How much uncertainty can I tolerate?
- Do I need structure or flexibility more?
- Am I rebuilding capacity or chasing identity?

There is no shame in choosing employment. There is no superiority in choosing entrepreneurship. There is no failure in choosing both. The rebuild succeeds when the choice matches reality.

Redefining "Success" During a Rebuild

Success during a rebuild looks different than success before collapse. It looks like:
- Paying bills without panic

- Sleeping better
- Making clearer decisions
- Showing up consistently
- Building confidence slowly
- Protecting energy

This season is not about proving anything. It is about stabilizing enough to grow again.

Practice: The Stability Path Decision

Write down:
- Your current financial needs
- Your emotional capacity
- Your risk tolerance
- Your available time and energy

Then choose the path that best supports:
- Stability
- Sustainability
- Health
- Forward motion

You are not locking yourself into this forever. You are choosing what supports the rebuild *now*.

Why This Chapter Matters

Many rebuilders delay progress because they believe the next step must define their future. It does not. Work is a tool. Income is infrastructure. Stability is the goal. When stability is established, identity expands. When pressure decreases, clarity increases. When fear recedes, opportunity becomes visible. In the next chapter, we'll move deeper into **building income intentionally**, how to grow stability without recreating burnout, and how to think about money as support rather than self-worth.

The rebuild continues... And now, it has footing.

CHAPTER 22

Financial Foundations
for Rebuilders

Simple, accessible economic stability frameworks

M oney is one of the quietest sources of pressure in a rebuild. It rarely
announces itself loudly, but it shapes every decision beneath the
surface. When finances are unclear, everything feels heavier:

- Decisions feel rushed
- Risk feels dangerous
- Rest feels irresponsible
- Planning feels pointless

This chapter is not about wealth-building. It is not about optimization. It is not about financial sophistication. It is about **stability**. Rebuilders do not need complex financial systems. They need **visibility, control, and margin**.

Why Financial Clarity Comes Before Financial Growth

Many rebuilders avoid their finances because:

- They associate money with past burnout
- They feel shame about mistakes

163

- They're afraid of what they'll see
- They don't feel "ready" to look

Avoidance feels protective. It is not. Avoidance keeps the nervous system activated. Visibility calms it. You cannot rebuild what you refuse to see.

The Goal Is Not Perfection

It's Predictability. Financial stability means:

- Knowing what's coming in
- Knowing what's going out
- Knowing what matters most right now
- Reducing surprise and panic

You are not trying to impress anyone. You are trying to sleep at night.

Foundation One: Income Visibility

The first step in financial rebuilding is not budgeting. It is awareness. Ask:

- What income do I have right now?
- How predictable is it?
- What is guaranteed?
- What is variable?

Write it down. No judgment. No comparison. Clarity replaces fear.

Foundation Two: Expense Grounding

Rebuilders often confuse *necessary* expenses with *habitual* ones. Separate expenses into three categories:

1. **Non-negotiable**: housing, food, utilities, transportation
2. **Stabilizing**: phone, internet, basic healthcare, work-related costs
3. **Optional for now**: subscriptions, extras, lifestyle padding

This is not deprivation. It is prioritization. Stability comes from knowing what truly matters.

Foundation Three: The "Enough" Number

Most people don't know how much they actually need. They either:
- Underestimate and panic
- Overestimate and feel trapped

Calculate your **minimum sustainable monthly number**:
- Enough to live
- Enough to function
- Enough to reduce stress

This is not your forever number. It is your *"now"* number. Knowing it gives you leverage.

Foundation Four: Weekly Money Check-Ins

Avoiding money creates anxiety. Obsessing over money creates anxiety. Consistency creates calm. Once a week, ask:
- What came in?
- What went out?
- What do I need to prepare for next week?

Ten minutes. Same day each week. Money stops feeling threatening when it becomes familiar.

Foundation Five: Buffer Before Growth

Rebuilders often rush toward financial goals:
- More income
- Better lifestyle
- Catching up
- Proving recovery

But growth without buffer recreates fragility. Before scaling:

- Build a small emergency margin. Try to build up to $500. Then set the goal of $1,000. Once at $1,000, work on your high-stress obligations. Once your high-stress debt is reduced, then set a goal to ultimately get to $10,000 as an emergency buffer.
- Reduce high-stress obligations. Start with your smallest debts. Each time you pay something off, add what you were paying to the next in line and keep going. Momentum is the key as financial stability grows.
- Stabilize cash flow. Keep your weekly check-in. Knowledge is power. Power will allow you to sleep at night.
- Protect basic needs. Your non-negotiables stay your non-negotiables.

A buffer is not excess. It is protection.

Financial Stability Without Shame

Many rebuilders carry financial shame:

- Past decisions
- Lost income
- Debt
- Missed opportunities
- Shame does not fix finances. Clarity does. Money is information.

Money is:

- **NOT identity.**
- **NOT morality.**
- **NOT worth.**

Your financial position is not a verdict. It is a starting point.

Practice: The Financial Grounding Exercise

This week, do the following:

1. Write down your current income sources
2. List your non-negotiable expenses
3. Identify your "enough for now" number
4. Schedule a weekly money check-in

That's it. You do not need to solve everything. You need to stabilize.

Why This Chapter Matters

Financial instability keeps rebuilders trapped in survival mode. Survival mode blocks clarity. Clarity blocks Urgency.

When finances stabilize:

- Decisions slow down
- Emotions settle
- Energy returns
- Options expand

Money becomes what it should have always been: **support, not stress**. In the next chapter, we'll look at **longer-term income pathways**, how stability evolves over time, and how to build toward sustainability without recreating the systems that caused collapse in the first place.

The rebuild continues… And now, it rests on firmer ground.

PART V

THE SYSTEM. HOW BUILT FOR REBUILDING WORKS

CHAPTER 23

The Built for Rebuilding Operating System

The Universal Sequence Every Rebuilder Moves Through

Rebuilding is not random. It feels chaotic while you're inside it, but beneath the surface, there is a pattern. Every rebuilder, regardless of background, failure, trauma, or circumstance, moves through the same **sequence**. What changes is not the order, but the pace, the depth, and the resistance at each stage.

Built for Rebuilding is **NOT** a mindset. It is **not** motivation. It is **not** inspiration. It is an **operating system**. An internal and external sequence that governs how rebuilding actually works when it lasts.

◊ Most rebuilds fail because people try to skip stages.

◊ They chase action before clarity.

◊ They pursue strategy before identity.

◊ They chase income before stability.

◊ They attempt growth while still fractured.

This chapter explains the system beneath everything you've read so far.

Why Rebuilding Needs an Operating System

When a life collapses, people instinctively ask:
- What should I do next?
- What's the fastest way out of this?
- How do I get back to where I was?

Those questions are understandable. They are also incomplete. Action without sequence recreates chaos. Speed without structure recreates burnout. Progress without alignment recreates collapse. An operating system does three things:

1. It defines **order**
2. It reduces **decision fatigue**
3. It creates **stability under stress**

Built for Rebuilding provides that system.

The Five-Stage Rebuilder Sequence

Every sustainable rebuild follows this order:

1. **Identity**
2. **Truth & Clarity**
3. **Tools & Skills**
4. **Structure & Strategy**
5. **Income & Stability**

You've already walked through these pillars. Now it's time to understand how they function **together**. This is not linear forever. But it is linear at the beginning.

Stage One: Identity

Who you are after what happened. Rebuilding always begins with identity, whether people realize it or not. Before you can decide what to do, you must understand:

- Who you are now
- What was stripped away
- What was never actually yours
- What remains true beneath the damage

Identity answers questions like:

- What do I value now?
- What will I no longer tolerate?
- What version of myself am I rebuilding from?

Skipping identity leads to false rebuilds. People recreate careers, relationships, or lifestyles that no longer fit, then wonder why they collapse again. Identity is the foundation. Everything else rests on it.

Stage Two: Truth & Clarity

Seeing reality without distortion or shame. Once identity stabilizes, truth becomes possible. Truth is not self-attack. Clarity is not punishment. This stage is about:

- Naming patterns honestly
- Seeing choices clearly
- Understanding limits without judgment
- Accepting responsibility without self-destruction

Truth allows rebuilders to stop lying to themselves in subtle ways:

- About capacity
- About readiness
- About motives
- About what is actually sustainable

Clarity replaces emotional guessing with grounded awareness. Without clarity, people build plans on fantasies. With clarity, they build on reality.

Stage Three: Tools & Skills

Learning how to function again. Once truth is established, tools become useful. Tools before clarity feel overwhelming. Tools after clarity feel empowering. This stage focuses on:

- Emotional regulation
- Mental frameworks
- Communication skills
- Planning basics
- Financial fundamentals
- Work and life competencies

Rebuilders do not need complexity. They need tools that work under pressure. Skills rebuild confidence. Tools rebuild agency. Agency rebuilds momentum.

Stage Four: Structure & Strategy

Turning effort into direction. This is where many rebuilders *think* they should start. It's why so many fail. Structure only works once the internal systems are stable. This stage answers:

- How do I sequence my days?
- What systems support me?
- What routines protect my energy?
- What strategies fit my current capacity?

Structure is not control. It is containment. It holds you steady while life moves around you. Strategy without identity is fragile. Strategy with structure becomes sustainable.

Stage Five: Income & Stability

Creating a foundation that can hold your life. Income is not the first pillar. But it is a non-negotiable one. This stage focuses on:

- Predictable income
- Financial grounding
- Employment or entrepreneurship pathways
- Reducing economic stress
- Building margin before growth

Income provides:

- Safety
- Choice
- Time
- Reduced pressure

Stability allows the nervous system to settle. When the nervous system settles, rebuilding accelerates.

How the System Actually Works in Real Life

Rebuilders do not move cleanly from one stage to the next. They:

- Loop back
- Stall
- Resist
- Revisit earlier stages under stress

The best thing is… that's normal. The operating system is not rigid. It is **responsive**. When something breaks, you don't push harder. You ask:

- Which stage am I skipping?
- What foundation is missing?
- What am I trying to build on top of instability?

The system gives you a diagnostic lens, not a judgment.

The Most Important Rule of the System

You cannot outwork misalignment. No amount of hustle fixes:

- A fractured identity
- Avoided truth
- Lack of tools
- Missing structure
- Financial chaos

Rebuilding works when effort aligns with sequence.

Practice: Locate Yourself in the System

Right now, ask yourself:

- Which stage am I strongest in?
- Which stage am I avoiding?
- Where do I feel the most resistance?

That's where the work is. You don't need to do everything. You need to do the **next right thing**, in the **right order**.

Why This System Matters

Built for Rebuilding is not about getting back to who you were. It is about building a life that:

- Fits who you are now
- Respects your limits
- Honors your truth
- Supports your stability
- Can withstand future stress

This system exists so you don't have to guess anymore. In the next chapter, we'll explore **how rebuilders move through this system over time**, what progress actually looks like, and how to recognize when you're ready to advance instead of forcing it.

The rebuild is no longer abstract… It has a structure. And now, you know how it works.

CHAPTER 24

The Tools, Frameworks, and Methods

How structure turns rebuilding into forward motion

B y this point in the book, something important should feel different. You are no longer asking, *"What's wrong with me?"* You are asking, *"What system will hold me as I rebuild?"*

That shift matters. Rebuilding does not fail because people lack motivation. It fails because motivation is asked to do the job of structure. This chapter introduces the **tools and frameworks** that support the Built for Rebuilding operating system. Not as a theory. Not as branding. But as **practical scaffolding** for people rebuilding real lives under real pressure. These tools exist for one reason: To translate dignity, truth, clarity, and intention into daily, sustainable action.

Tools Are Not the Work. They Support the Work.

Before we go further, one clarification matters. Tools do not rebuild your life. Frameworks do not heal identity. Methods do not replace responsibility. What they *do* is reduce friction. They:

- Create order where chaos lives
- Reduce decision fatigue
- Prevent emotional overwhelm from hijacking progress
- Turn insight into execution

Think of tools as **rails**, not engines. They don't move you forward on their own, but without them, momentum derails easily.

The Three Core Frameworks of Built for Rebuilding

Built for Rebuilding is supported by three integrated frameworks:

1. **The Building Understanding Process**
2. **The Business Clarity Protocol**
3. **The Business Blueprint Model**

Each serves a different purpose, and each comes into play at a different stage of the rebuild. They are not used all at once. They are introduced **when the foundation can support them**.

Framework One: The Building Understanding Process

Understanding what you are actually building. Despite the name, the Building Understanding Process is not just for entrepreneurs. It is a **clarity framework** for anyone rebuilding work, income, or purpose. At its core, the framework answers five essential questions:

- What am I building?
- Who is it for?
- Why does it exist?
- How does it function?
- What must be true for it to succeed?

For rebuilders, this framework is powerful because it prevents premature action.

Instead of rushing into:

- The next job
- The next business idea
- The next opportunity
- The next "fix"

This process forces clarity **before commitment**. It helps rebuilders:

- Avoid rebuilding the wrong thing
- Align work with identity
- Understand trade-offs honestly
- Build from capacity, not fantasy

This framework belongs **after identity and clarity**, not before.

Framework Two: The Business Clarity Protocol

Stabilizing before scaling. Again, while the title says business, the protocol fits work, career, and daily life. Where the Building Understanding Process defines *what* you're building, the Business Clarity Protocol governs **how you rebuild without burning out again**. This protocol exists because many rebuilders are capable, driven, and intelligent, but exhausted, dysregulated, or operating from survival. The Clarity Protocol focuses on:

- Stabilizing operations
- Clarifying priorities
- Removing hidden friction
- Rebuilding confidence through execution
- Creating margin before growth

It is especially effective for:

- Entrepreneurs at zero
- Professionals starting over
- Founders exiting survival mode
- Justice-impacted rebuilders navigating limited options

The protocol emphasizes:

- Fewer priorities
- Clear sequencing
- Realistic capacity
- Sustainable pacing

This is where rebuilders learn that **clarity is an operational advantage**, not a luxury.

Framework Three: The Business Blueprint Model

Turning long-term vision into daily stability. Most people fail at execution for one simple reason: **They cannot connect the future to today.** Vision feels abstract. Daily life feels heavy. The gap becomes paralysis. The Business Blueprint Model closes that gap. While the name is Business Blueprint, the lessons and structure can be applied to every facet of life.

It operates on six levels:

1. **Vision** (10–15 years)
2. **Mission** (3–5 years)
3. **Annual Focus** (yearly)
4. **Strategy** (6-months)
5. **Tactics** (3-months)
6. **Daily Actions**

Rebuilders do not live in the future. They live in today.

This model ensures that:

- Daily actions are purposeful
- Effort is not wasted
- Progress is visible
- Identity aligns with behavior

When rebuilders know *why* today matters, they stop drifting.

How These Tools Work Together

These frameworks are not separate programs. They are **stacked intentionally**.

- The **Building Understanding Process** creates clarity of direction.
- The **Business Clarity Protocol** stabilizes execution.
- The **Business Blueprint Model** sustains momentum.

Together, they prevent:

- Overplanning
- Overworking
- Overcommitting
- Recreating collapse through misalignment

They support the operating system without replacing human judgment.

Tools Without Identity Create Fragile Rebuilds

One warning matters here. If tools are used:

- Before dignity is restored
- Before truth is faced
- Before agency is reclaimed
- Before internal stability exists

They become weapons against the self. This book intentionally placed tools **after identity, clarity, and stability** for a reason. When the self is grounded, tools empower. When the self is fractured, tools overwhelm.

Practice: Choosing the Right Tool at the Right Time

Ask yourself:

- Am I seeking clarity or execution?

- Do I need direction or stability?
- Am I building something new or repairing something broken?
- Am I planning for my future?

The answer determines the tool. Rebuilding is not about using *all* frameworks. It's about using the **right one**, at the **right moment**, for the **right reason**.

The Real Purpose of These Frameworks

These tools exist to do one thing well: **Help you rebuild a life that doesn't require you to break again to sustain it.**

- They are not about speed.
- They are not about optimization.
- They are not about hustle.

They are about alignment, capacity, and durability. In the next chapter, we'll step back and look at **how rebuilders progress over time**, what real momentum looks like, and how to recognize when growth is healthy versus reactive.

The tools are here… Now it's about using them wisely.

CHAPTER 25

The Ecosystem: Courses, Community, Coaching, Books, and More

How rebuilding is supported at every level, for every season.

Rebuilding is not a single decision. It is not a moment of clarity. It is not a breakthrough that permanently fixes everything. Rebuilding is a process.

It unfolds over time, in layers, through seasons of strength and seasons of strain. And no matter how capable a person is, rebuilding alone is one of the fastest ways to stall, burn out, or quietly give up. This chapter explains the **Built for Rebuilding ecosystem**. Not as a product list. Not as a funnel. But as a **support structure** designed to meet people where they actually are and walk with them as they move forward. Because rebuilding does not happen at one level. It happens across many.

Why an Ecosystem Matters

Most people seeking change encounter one of two broken models:

- **Inspiration without support**, motivation with nowhere to land
- **Information without context**, tools handed to people who are not ready to use them

Built for Rebuilding exists because neither model works. An ecosystem matters because:

- People rebuild at different speeds
- Capacity fluctuates
- Needs change as stability grows
- Identity, clarity, skills, and income do not develop in a straight line

The ecosystem exists to provide **continuity**, not pressure. No one is expected to use everything. Everyone is supported somewhere.

The Five Layers of the Built for Rebuilding Ecosystem

The ecosystem is intentionally layered, not hierarchical. Each layer serves a distinct purpose and can stand alone, while also integrating with the others.

1. **Books and Written Work**
2. **Courses and Education**
3. **Community**
4. **Coaching and Advisory**
5. **Ongoing Resources and Expansion**

Each layer meets a different kind of need.

Layer One: Books and Written Work

Clarity you can return to. Books are often where rebuilding begins:

- They are private.

- They are self-paced.
- They allow reflection without exposure.
- They give language to experiences people struggle to name.

The books in the Built for Rebuilding ecosystem exist to:

- Normalize collapse without glorifying it
- Offer frameworks without pressure
- Create clarity without judgment
- Give readers a place to start when everything feels overwhelming

Books are not designed to "fix" someone. They are designed to **orient** someone. They give readers:

- Perspective
- Vocabulary
- Direction
- Permission to rebuild differently

For many, this is the safest entry point.

Layer Two: Courses and Education

Turning insight into skill. Reading creates understanding. Education creates capability. Courses exist for rebuilders who are ready to move from reflection into application, but still need structure and pacing. Built for Rebuilding courses are designed to be:

- Simple
- Practical
- Grounded
- Modular

They avoid:

- Jargon
- Hustle culture
- Over-optimization

- Performative productivity

Courses help rebuilders:

- Learn foundational skills
- Build confidence through competence
- Practice without pressure
- Progress without overwhelm

Education is not about proving intelligence. It is about building stability.

Layer Three: Community

Rebuilding without isolation. Collapse isolates people.

- Shame isolates people.
- Stigma isolates people.
- Starting over isolates people.

Community exists to counter that isolation. The Built for Rebuilding community is not built around hype, competition, or constant visibility. It is built around:

- Shared honesty
- Mutual respect
- Quiet accountability
- Psychological safety

Community provides:

- Normalization of struggle
- Shared language
- Perspective beyond self-blame
- Momentum through belonging

People don't rebuild because they're watched. They rebuild because they're **seen.**

Layer Four: Coaching and Advisory

Personalized support when the stakes are higher. Some rebuilders reach a point where general guidance is no longer enough. They need:

- Individual attention
- Strategic feedback
- Accountability with compassion
- Help navigating complexity

Coaching and advisory exist for rebuilders who:

- Are making consequential decisions
- Are rebuilding businesses or careers
- Are navigating leadership, operations, or growth
- Need help stabilizing before scaling

This layer is not about dependency. It is about **compression of learning** and avoidance of preventable mistakes. The goal is always autonomy. Support is temporary. Capability is permanent.

Layer Five: Ongoing Resources and Expansion

Support that evolves as life evolves.

Rebuilding does not end when stability returns. Life continues to change. New challenges appear. Different seasons require different tools. The ecosystem is designed to grow with the rebuilder, offering:

- Advanced tools
- Deeper frameworks
- Specialized education
- Expanded community pathways

Not to keep people inside a system, but to ensure they are **not abandoned once things start working**.

How the Ecosystem Supports Different Rebuilders

Not everyone enters the ecosystem the same way.

- Some begin with a book during a quiet crisis.
- Some arrive through community after isolation.
- Some enter through coaching when the cost of mistakes is too high.
- Some move in and out of different layers over time.

There is no correct path. The ecosystem adapts to the person, not the other way around.

What This Ecosystem Is Not

It is not:

- A ladder you must climb
- A program you must complete
- A brand you must buy into
- A performance you must maintain

There is no "graduation" from rebuilding. There is only movement toward stability, dignity, and alignment.

The Deeper Purpose of the Ecosystem

At its core, the Built for Rebuilding ecosystem exists to answer one question: **What does support look like when rebuilding is treated as a human process, not a personal failure?** The answer is:

- Options instead of pressure
- Structure instead of chaos
- Community instead of isolation
- Tools instead of shame
- Guidance instead of guessing

Rebuilding does not require perfection. It requires support that meets reality.

You Are Not Meant to Do This Alone

This chapter exists to make one thing clear: If you are rebuilding, needing help does not mean you are failing. It means you are rebuilding honestly. Whether you engage with one layer or many, whether you stay close or step away and return later, the ecosystem exists for one reason: To ensure that when you decide to rebuild, there is **something there to catch you**. In the final chapter of this book, we will step back and speak directly to the rebuilder, not with frameworks or systems, but with a reminder of what this entire journey is ultimately about.

Not rebuilding faster. Not rebuilding bigger... But rebuilding **true**.

PART VI

THE READER'S REBUILD. HOW THIS WORKS FOR YOU

CHAPTER 26

Naming Your Starting Point

*Your identity, your truth,
your pain point, your turning point*

E very rebuild begins in the same place. Not with a plan. Not with
motivation. Not with certainty.

It begins with **honest orientation**.

Before you decide what to build, you must name where you are
standing. Not where you wish you were. Not where others think you
should be. Where you actually are, right now, in this season of your
life. This chapter is about slowing down long enough to tell the truth
about your starting point, without judgment, without dramatizing
it, and without minimizing it. Because rebuilding without orientation creates confusion. And confusion quietly destroys momentum.

Why Naming the Starting Point Matters

Most people rush past this step. They jump into action because
stillness feels uncomfortable. They chase clarity because uncertainty
feels threatening. They adopt strategies meant for someone else's life

because facing their own reality feels too heavy. But rebuilding is not about speed. It is about accuracy. If you misname your starting point:

- You choose tools you are not ready for
- You chase outcomes that do not fit your reality
- You confuse effort with progress
- You punish yourself for results you were never positioned to achieve

Naming your starting point is not weakness. It is leadership of the self.

Four Things You Must Name to Begin

There are four truths every rebuilder must face honestly. Not all at once. Not perfectly. But clearly enough to move forward with integrity.

1. **Your current identity**
2. **Your lived truth**
3. **Your primary pain point**
4. **Your turning point**

These are not labels. They are coordinates.

1. Naming Your Current Identity

Who you are right now, not who you used to be. Identity after collapse often feels fragmented. You may feel like:

- A former version of yourself no longer fits
- A future version feels out of reach
- The present version feels unfamiliar or unfinished

This is normal. Rebuilding does not begin with reclaiming an old identity or inventing a new one. It begins with naming the one that exists right now. Ask yourself:

- Who am I in this season?

- What roles am I currently carrying?
- What parts of me feel stable?
- What parts feel uncertain or strained?

This is not about judgment. It is about acknowledgment. You cannot rebuild what you refuse to see.

Practice: Identity Snapshot

Write one paragraph that begins with:

"Right now, I am a person who…"

Do not explain. Do not justify. Do not soften the truth. Just name it.

2. Naming Your Truth

What is real beneath the stories? Truth is not the story you tell others. It is the reality you live with when no one is watching. This is clarity without shame. Truth includes:

- What hurts
- What you are avoiding
- What you are grieving
- What you are pretending doesn't matter
- What you are exhausted from carrying

Naming your truth does not make it heavier. It makes it clearer. Unspoken truth leaks into decisions, relationships, and self-perception. Spoken truth creates space for movement. Ask yourself:

- What am I actually dealing with right now?
- What feels unsustainable?
- What truth have I been postponing?

Practice: Truth Statement

Complete this sentence honestly:

"The truth about my life right now is…"

Write it once. Then stop. Truth does not require elaboration to be valid.

3. Naming Your Primary Pain Point

The pressure that is shaping your decisions. Collapse often creates many problems at once. But rebuilding requires focus. Your primary pain point is the issue that is:

- Draining the most energy
- Creating the most instability
- Quietly influencing your decisions
- Making everything else harder

It might be:

- Financial insecurity
- Loss of direction
- Identity confusion
- Burnout
- Shame
- Isolation
- Fear of making the wrong move
- A system working against you

This is not about ranking suffering. It is about identifying leverage. When the primary pain point is addressed, momentum follows.

Practice: Pain Point Clarity

Answer this question in one sentence:

"The one issue that, if stabilized,
would change everything else is…"

Do not list ten things… Name one.

4. Naming Your Turning Point

Why you are here now? Every rebuild has a moment, quiet or loud, when something shifted.

- A realization.
- A breaking point.
- A refusal to continue as things were.
- A sense that staying the same costs more than changing.

This is your turning point. It does not have to be dramatic. It just has to be true. Ask yourself:

- What made me open this book?
- What am I no longer willing to tolerate?
- What am I ready to face now that I wasn't before?

The turning point is not the solution. It is the signal.

Practice: Turning Point Marker

Complete this sentence:

"I am here because I can no longer…"

This sentence is not negative. It is directional.

What You Are Really Doing Here?

When you name your starting point, you are not defining your future. You are **locating yourself honestly** so that the rebuild can be built on solid ground instead of wishful thinking.

- ◊ This is dignity work.
- ◊ This is clarity work.
- ◊ This is leadership of the self.
- ◊ You are not behind.
- ◊ You are not broken.

◊ You are not late.

You are simply here. And here is enough to begin.

Moving Forward From Here

In the next chapter, we will begin translating your starting point into a **personal rebuild map**, one that respects your capacity, your constraints, and your humanity.

◊ No pressure.

◊ No comparison.

◊ No pretending.

Just the next honest step. That is how rebuilding actually works.

CHAPTER 27

Building Your Rebuild Plan

A structured guide readers can complete as they read.

Rebuilding does not happen through inspiration alone.
◊ Insight matters.

◊ Clarity matters.

◊ Hope matters.

But rebuilding requires **structure**.

◊ Without structure, insight fades.

◊ Without structure, motivation spikes and collapses.

◊ Without structure, rebuilders blame themselves for what was actually a missing plan.

This chapter turns everything you've learned so far into something concrete.

◊ Not a rigid blueprint.

◊ Not a five-year master plan.

◊ Not a fantasy version of your future.

This is a **rebuild plan**. Grounded. Flexible. Human. Designed to meet you where you are, not where you think you should be. You will not finish this chapter with everything solved. You will finish it with **direction**.

What a Rebuild Plan Is (and Is Not)

A rebuild plan is:

- A working document, not a fixed contract
- A sequence, not a pile of goals
- A stabilizing tool, not a pressure device
- A guide for decision-making when emotions run high
- A way to replace chaos with intention

A rebuild plan is not:

- A performance test
- A productivity contest
- A comparison to anyone else's life
- A guarantee against difficulty
- A demand for perfection

Your rebuild plan exists to answer these questions clearly: *"What am I building next, and how will I build it without breaking myself again?"*

The Five-Part Rebuild Plan

Your rebuild plan mirrors the Five Pillars and the rebuild pathway you've already learned. This is your minimum effective structure:

1. Identity Anchor
2. Truth & Clarity Focus
3. Tools & Skills Priorities
4. Structure & Strategy Path
5. Stability Targets

You will complete each part in order. Do not skip ahead. Each section depends on the one before it.

Part 1: Your Identity Anchor

Who you are rebuilding as? Before you define goals, you must define **who you are becoming**. This anchor keeps the rebuild aligned when pressure, fear, or opportunity tries to pull you off course.

Your Identity Anchor Statement

Complete the following:

"In this rebuild, I am committed
to becoming a person who…"

Examples:

- "…rebuilds slowly and sustainably."
- "…chooses truth over appearance."
- "…protects their mental and emotional health."
- "…builds stability before chasing growth."
- "…leads themselves with dignity."

Now answer:

- What behaviors support this identity?
- What behaviors violate it?

Write both. This becomes your internal filter for future decisions.

Part 2: Your Truth & Clarity Focus

What must be addressed first? Rebuilders fail when they try to fix everything at once. Clarity comes from **choosing focus**.

Identify Your Primary Focus Area

Answer this honestly:

"The one area of my life that requires
my primary attention right now is…"

Common answers include:

- Income and financial stability
- Emotional regulation and mental health
- Career direction or employment
- Business foundation or relaunch
- Housing, safety, or basic stability
- Identity and confidence rebuilding

Now answer:

- Why is this the priority?
- What happens if this remains unresolved?

This is not about urgency alone. It is about leverage.

Part 3: Your Tools & Skills Priorities

What you actually need to learn or strengthen? Most rebuilders overwhelm themselves with tools they do not need yet. Your rebuild plan focuses on **capability over complexity**.

Choose 3 Core Skills to Build

Answer:

> "The three skills that would most stabilize
> or strengthen my life right now are…"

Examples:

- Emotional regulation
- Decision-making
- Communication
- Financial basics
- Time and energy management
- Job search skills
- Business fundamentals
- Boundary-setting

For each skill, write:
- Why it matters now
- One simple way to practice it weekly

This prevents overlearning and underapplying.

Part 4: Your Structure & Strategy Path

How the rebuild will move forward? Structure turns intention into progress. This section defines **how you will move**, not how fast.

Define Your Rebuild Phase

Circle one:
- Stabilizing
- Resetting
- Rebuilding
- Expanding

Now answer:
- What does success look like in this phase?
- What does "too much" look like in this phase?

Weekly Structure Snapshot

Define:
- One priority focus per week
- One non-negotiable self-care practice
- One action that supports stability

This becomes your **minimum viable structure**. If nothing else happens, this still counts as progress.

Part 5: Your Stability Targets

What stability looks like for you? Stability is not perfection. It is predictability and safety.

Define Stability in Three Areas

Complete the following:

1. **Emotional Stability**

   "I will know I am more stable emotionally when…"

2. **Practical Stability**

   "I will know I am more stable practically when…"

3. **Financial Stability**

   "I will know I am more stable financially when…"

Do not aim for ideal. Aim for **better than now**.

The One-Page Rebuild Plan Summary

At the end of this chapter, you should be able to summarize your rebuild plan in one page:

- Who you are rebuilding as
- What you are focusing on first
- What skills you are strengthening
- How you will structure your weeks
- What stability looks like right now

If it cannot fit on one page, it is too complex.

A Final Word on Pace and Permission

Your rebuild plan does not need to impress anyone. It needs to **hold you**.

◊ You are allowed to move slowly.

◊ You are allowed to revise the plan.

◊ You are allowed to rest without guilt.

◊ You are allowed to change direction with honesty.

A rebuild plan is not a promise to never struggle again. It is a promise to yourself that you will not abandon yourself again... That promise is enough. In the next chapter, we will address **what gets in the way of following your plan**, fear, setbacks, old patterns, and external pressure, and how to stay grounded when rebuilding stops feeling clean or linear.

Because rebuilding is not about avoiding difficulty... It is about staying aligned when difficulty shows up.

CHAPTER 28

The First 30 Days

A simple, powerful sequence for beginning the rebuild today

Rebuilding does not start with a grand gesture... It starts with **today**. Not when you feel ready. Not when you have clarity. Not when fear quiets down.

The first 30 days are not about fixing your life. They are about **stabilizing yourself**. This chapter gives you a clear, humane sequence you can follow without overwhelm. No intensity. No hustle. No pressure to "prove" anything. Just enough structure to help you stand back up.

What the First 30 Days Are For

This is your minimum effective month. These first 30 days exist to do four things:

1. Interrupt collapse patterns
2. Restore internal stability
3. Build early evidence of agency
4. Create momentum without burnout

They are not for:

- Reinvention
- Big decisions
- Major commitments
- Life-altering risks

If you treat these 30 days as a performance, you will exhaust yourself. If you treat them as **practice**, you will begin to rebuild.

The 30-Day Rebuild Rhythm

Each week has a single focus. Each day has **one primary action…** That's it.

Weekly Focus Overview

- **Week 1:** Stabilize the Nervous System
- **Week 2:** Restore Agency Through Action
- **Week 3:** Rebuild Identity Through Consistency
- **Week 4:** Establish Structure That Holds

You are not racing the calendar. You are reclaiming yourself.

WEEK 1: STABILIZE FIRST

Days 1–7: Creating internal safety

Before clarity, before plans, before goals, the body and mind must calm. Collapse keeps people in reaction mode. This week is about slowing the internal storm.

Daily Non-Negotiables (Every Day This Week)

- Wake up at roughly the same time
- Eat at least two real meals
- Drink water intentionally

- Go outside for at least 10 minutes
- Sleep without self-punishment

This is not self-care fluff. This is **foundational regulation**.

Daily Practice

Each day, do the **3-Breath Reset** at least three times:
- Once in the morning
- Once before a decision
- Once when emotionally triggered

Write this sentence each night:

"Today, my body needed ___, and I honored that."

Stability begins when your nervous system feels safe enough to think again.

WEEK 2: RESTORE AGENCY

Days 8–14: Rebuilding self-trust through choice

Agency returns through **action**, not confidence. This week proves to you that you can still choose. Continue practicing your daily non-negotiables and 3-breath resets, then:

The One-Choice Rule

Each morning, answer:

"What is one thing I will choose today, not collapse?"

Examples:
- Take a walk
- Apply for one job
- Make one phone call
- Clean one surface
- Tell one truth

Do not stack choices. One is enough.

Daily Reflection

Each night, write:

"Today, I chose ___ even though I felt ___."

This rebuilds self-trust quietly and powerfully. Tomorrow, try a different choice.

WEEK 3: REBUILD IDENTITY

Days 15–21: Becoming consistent instead of intense

Identity does not rebuild through insight. It rebuilds through **patterns**. This week focuses on showing yourself who you are becoming. Continue your non-negotiables and 3-breath resets from week 1. Continue your nightly reflection of one choice you made for intentional agency restoration. Now:

Identity-in-Action Practice

Choose **one identity statement**:
- "I am someone who finishes what matters."
- "I am someone who tells the truth."
- "I am someone who rebuilds sustainably."
- "I am someone who respects my limits."

Each day, do **one small action** that proves it. Examples:
- Finish a small task
- Speak honestly
- Stop when tired
- Keep a simple commitment

Evidence Journal (Nightly)

Write:

"Today I proved to myself that I am becoming someone who ___."

Belief follows evidence. Not the other way around.

WEEK 4: ESTABLISH STRUCTURE

Days 22–30: Turning momentum into stability

Now that you are steadier, it's time to add **light structure**. Not a rigid plan. A container.

Create a Simple Weekly Framework

Write down:
- One focus for the week
- One daily anchor habit
- One rest boundary
- One action that supports income or stability

This is your **minimum viable structure**.

The Weekly Review (Day 30)

Answer honestly:
- What helped me feel more grounded?
- What drained me unnecessarily?
- What patterns do I want to keep?
- What needs to change next month?

Clarity grows through reflection, not force.

If You Miss a Day

You did not fail. You are rebuilding. You resume the next day without punishment, explanation, or shame. Consistency beats perfection… EVERY TIME.

What You Should Feel After 30 days

Not fixed. Not fearless. Not "back." You should feel:

- More grounded
- Less reactive
- Clearer about what matters
- More trusting of yourself
- Capable of continuing

That is success.

A Closing Truth

The first 30 days are not about becoming impressive. They are about becoming **steady**. From steadiness comes clarity. From clarity comes direction. From direction comes rebuilding that lasts.

You have already begun.

In the next chapter, we'll address **what threatens momentum**, fear, setbacks, old identities, and external pressure, and how to stay aligned when rebuilding stops feeling clean or hopeful.

Because the real work isn't starting… It's **continuing**.

PART VII

PURPOSE & IMPACT.
THE REBUILD BEYOND YOU

CHAPTER 29

The Power of Second Chances

Why rebuilding is never only about you

R ebuilding begins as a deeply personal act. It starts in private moments, quiet decisions, and internal reckonings no one else sees. But if rebuilding stops there, it remains incomplete. Every meaningful rebuild eventually turns outward.

Not as obligation. Not as repayment. But as purpose.

Second chances are not just personal resets.

◊ They are **social acts**.

◊ They change families.

◊ They reshape communities.

◊ They interrupt cycles that would otherwise repeat.

This chapter is about what happens when your rebuild moves beyond survival and into meaning.

Second Chances Are How Systems Change

Most systems are built around first impressions.

◊ One mistake.

◊ One failure.

◊ One label.

◊ One moment frozen in time.

But real life doesn't work that way.

◊ People evolve.

◊ Context matters.

◊ Growth happens unevenly.

◊ Healing takes time.

Second chances are the mechanism through which systems regain their humanity. When someone is allowed to rebuild, the system itself becomes more honest.

Why Second Chances Matter More Than Success Stories

We celebrate success narratives because they feel clean. But second chances are messy. They involve:

- Accountability without erasure
- Growth without applause
- Progress without guarantees

Second chances don't erase responsibility. They create **room for transformation**. A culture that believes in second chances is not soft… It is realistic. Because people are not static. And neither are their futures.

The Hidden Truth: You Are Someone Else's Second Chance

Whether you realize it or not, your rebuild is already impacting others. When you:

◊ Choose honesty over hiding

◊ Choose steadiness over chaos

◊ Choose dignity over shame

◊ Choose consistency over intensity

You create permission.

◊ Someone is watching you decide not to quit.

◊ Someone is watching you rebuild without self-destruction.

◊ Someone is watching you choose integrity when it would be easier not to.

Second chances ripple outward.

From Personal Healing to Collective Impact

Purpose doesn't arrive as a calling. It arrives as alignment. It shows up when:

- Your pain becomes insight
- Your experience becomes guidance
- Your survival becomes structure for others
- You don't need to lead a movement.
- You don't need a platform.
- You don't need to be "fixed."

You only need to be **honest about what you've lived** and intentional about how you live now. Impact grows naturally from that place.

Why Rebuilders See the World Differently

People who have rebuilt don't romanticize systems. They understand:

- How easily people fall through cracks
- How labels replace nuance

- How shame delays healing
- How support changes outcomes

Rebuilders don't ask, *"Who deserves a second chance?"* They ask, *"What does rebuilding actually require?"*

That question changes everything.

Second Chances Are Not Charity

They are not favors. They are not exceptions… They are investments. When people are allowed to rebuild with dignity, society gains:

- Stability
- Contribution
- Leadership
- Insight
- Compassion grounded in reality

Second chances are not about ignoring the past. They are about **refusing to let the past be the final word.**

The Quiet Responsibility of Rebuilding

No one owes the world perfection. But rebuilders carry a quiet responsibility: **To not waste what collapse taught them.** That doesn't mean carrying guilt… It means carrying awareness.

- You know what it costs to fall.
- You know what it takes to rise.
- You know what makes rebuilding harder than it needs to be.

That knowledge matters.

A Rebuild That Extends Beyond You

Eventually, every rebuilder reaches a crossroads. You can:

- Protect your new life fiercely and stop there, or
- Let your rebuilt life become a bridge for others

Neither choice is wrong. But one choice turns rebuilding into legacy. Second chances are how legacy is formed. Not through titles. Not through success. But through **access, grace, and truth**.

A Final Reflection

Ask yourself:
- Who believed in me when I didn't?
- Who withheld belief when I needed it most?
- What made my rebuild harder than it needed to be?
- What made it possible anyway?

Your answers point directly to your purpose. Because the rebuild beyond you is not about saving others. It's about **removing unnecessary barriers** so rebuilding becomes possible at all. In the next chapter, we'll explore how purpose takes shape not as pressure, but as direction, and how rebuilders create meaning without burning themselves out trying to "give back."

The rebuild continues. But now, it carries weight.

CHAPTER 30

Sidre: Rebuilding in the Real World

Jobs, skills, training, stability, and justice with dignity

Rebuilding is easy to talk about in theory. It becomes real when rent is due. When background checks close doors. When skills are outdated. When gaps in work history raise questions. When stigma follows you into every interview, application, and conversation.

This is where rebuilding either becomes possible... or collapses again.

Sidre exists for this exact moment. Not as inspiration. Not as charity. But as **infrastructure for real-world rebuilding**.

Why Real-World Rebuilding Requires More Than Motivation

Motivation doesn't overcome systemic barriers. Hope doesn't create or replace income. Positive thinking doesn't secure housing. People don't fail to rebuild because they lack desire. They fail because the world is not designed to let them rise easily once they fall. Sidre was built to meet Justice-Impacted rebuilders **where theory ends and reality begins**.

Rebuilding With Dignity, Not Dependency

Sidre's work is grounded in one non-negotiable belief: **People are not broken; systems are.** Rebuilding does not mean rescuing. It means **restoring access.** Sidre does not lower standards. It raises support. It does not excuse responsibility. It creates conditions where responsibility can actually be lived out.

The Real Barriers Justice-Impacted Rebuilders Face

For justice-impacted individuals especially, rebuilding means navigating obstacles most people never see:
- Employment restrictions
- Housing discrimination
- Financial instability
- Limited access to education or training
- Mental health challenges
- Family reintegration
- Ongoing surveillance or supervision
- Internalized shame

These are not personal failures. They are structural realities. Sidre addresses them directly.

The Fundamentals of Sidre's Real-World Rebuild

Sidre focuses on five practical areas, all rooted in dignity.

1. Employment That Leads Somewhere

Work is not just income. It is identity, rhythm, and belonging. Sidre helps rebuilders:
- Prepare for employment honestly and strategically
- Build resumes that tell the truth without self-erasure

- Develop interview confidence grounded in reality
- Connect with second-chance employers who value contribution

Employment is treated as a foundation, not a finish line.

2. Skill-Building That Creates Mobility

Many rebuilders are capable but under-credentialed. Others are credentialed but locked out. Sidre focuses on:

- Transferable skills
- Practical training
- Business fundamentals
- Financial literacy
- Entrepreneurial pathways when employment access is limited

Skills restore agency. Agency restores momentum.

3. Stability Before Ambition

Sidre does not push people to "dream big" before they can stand steady. The priority is:

- Housing stability
- Income predictability
- Routine and structure
- Emotional regulation
- Support systems

Ambition without stability becomes self-destruction. Sidre rebuilds the base first.

4. Justice With Humanity

Sidre operates with a clear-eyed understanding of the justice system. It does not ignore accountability. It refuses lifelong punishment. Sidre advocates for:

- Fair access to opportunity
- Dignity in reentry
- Policy awareness
- Employer education
- Community reintegration

Justice should restore, not permanently exclude.

5. Community as a Protective Factor

Isolation is one of the most dangerous threats to rebuilding. Sidre creates community that:

- Normalizes the rebuild process
- Reduces shame
- Encourages consistency
- Reinforces dignity
- Shares lived wisdom

People rebuild faster and stronger when they are not alone.

Why Sidre Is the Heart of Built for Rebuilding

Sidre exists for the rebuilders facing the steepest climb. Those who:

- Want to work but are denied access
- Want to contribute but are locked out
- Want to rebuild but are carrying labels the world won't release

Sidre ensures that Built for Rebuilding never becomes abstract.

- It keeps the mission honest.
- It keeps the work grounded.
- It keeps dignity at the center.

Rebuilding That Changes the World Quietly

Sidre does not promise miracles. It promises **pathways**. It does not market hope. It builds structure.

Every person who rebuilds with dignity:

- Reduces cycles of harm
- Strengthens families
- Stabilizes communities
- Adds leadership forged in reality

This is how change actually happens.

A Final Truth

Rebuilding is not a personal luxury. It is a social necessity. When people are denied the ability to rebuild, everyone pays the cost. When people are supported in rebuilding, everyone benefits. Sidre exists to prove one thing in the real world:

Second chances are not just possible. They are practical. They are necessary. And they work.

In the final chapter, we'll bring everything together, the philosophy, the pillars, the system, and your path forward, and close with a clear truth:

Your rebuild matters... And it was never meant to stop with you.

CHAPTER 31

Rebuilding as Identity, Community, and Movement

The broader mission behind Built for Rebuilding

R ebuilding is often framed as a temporary phase. Something you
do until things "get better." Something you endure until life stabilizes again. But that framing misses something essential. For many of
us, rebuilding is not a chapter. It is an identity. It is a way of moving
through the world. It is a lens through which we see systems, people,
failure, and possibility.

Built for Rebuilding was never meant to be a momentary inter-
vention. It was designed as a **way of living**, a **way of belonging**, and
eventually, a **way of changing the world**.

Rebuilding as Identity

When you have rebuilt your life, truly rebuilt it, something
permanent changes. You no longer believe the myths:
- That worth is fragile
- That failure is final

227

- That people are static
- That systems are always right

Rebuilders carry a different kind of awareness. They understand that identity is not fixed by titles, income, status, or mistakes. They know that collapse does not disqualify a person, it reveals what matters. To be a rebuilder is to live with:

- Humility earned, not performed
- Strength tested, not assumed
- Compassion grounded in reality
- Truth without illusion

Rebuilding becomes part of who you are, not because you enjoy hardship, but because you know survival is not the same as living.

Rebuilding as Community

Rebuilding is dangerous in isolation. Shame grows in silence. Distortion thrives alone. Momentum dies without witnesses. That is why Built for Rebuilding is not built around heroes. It is built around **people**. Community is not a bonus feature. It is a stabilizing force. In rebuilding communities:

- Progress is normalized
- Setbacks are contextualized
- Accountability is humane
- Growth is modeled, not demanded

People don't gather because they are broken. They gather because they are becoming. Community reminds rebuilders:

- You are not late.
- You are not weak.
- You are not alone.
- You are not disqualified.

Rebuilding as Movement

Movements don't begin with slogans. They begin with shared truth. Built for Rebuilding is not a protest movement. It is a **restorative one**. It challenges:

- Permanent punishment
- Disposable people
- Shame-based systems
- Productivity-as-worth culture
- One-strike narratives

Not with outrage. With structure. Not with blame. With pathways. When enough people rebuild with dignity, the culture has to change. Not because it wants to, but because reality demands it. Movements form when lived experience becomes collective insight.

What This Movement Is Not

Built for Rebuilding is not:

- Anti-accountability
- Anti-work
- Anti-structure
- Anti-success

It is:

- Aanti-shame.
- Anti-finality.

It believes:

- People are more than their worst moment.
- People grow when given access.
- Stability creates contribution.
- Dignity changes outcomes.

The Quiet Power of Rebuilders

Rebuilders rarely announce themselves.

- They show up differently.
- They lead differently.
- They listen more.
- They rush less.
- They build with intention.

They become:

- Employers who give access
- Leaders who create safety
- Mentors who tell the truth
- Neighbors who don't look away
- Parents who break cycles

Rebuilders don't dominate spaces. They stabilize them.

Your Place in the Movement

- You don't have to adopt a label.
- You don't have to join a cause.
- You don't have to carry a banner.

You are already part of this if:

- You refuse to reduce people to their mistakes
- You build systems that can hold real lives
- You lead with dignity under pressure
- You allow growth without humiliation

Every rebuild lived with integrity becomes proof that another way is possible.

A Living Mission

Built for Rebuilding is not finished. It evolves with the people inside it.

As long as:

- People fall through cracks
- Systems confuse punishment with justice
- Identity is reduced to productivity
- Shame is mistaken for accountability

Rebuilding will remain necessary. And so will this work.

A Closing Reflection

Ask yourself:

- How has rebuilding changed how I see people?
- Where do I now create space instead of judgment?
- What systems do I interact with differently because of what I've lived?
- How might my rebuild quietly give someone else permission to begin?

You don't have to save the world. You just have to live your rebuild honestly. That is how identity becomes community. That is how community becomes movement. That is how rebuilding reshapes the future.

In the final chapter, we'll bring this journey to a close, not with an ending, but with an invitation:

To keep rebuilding.

To keep choosing dignity.

And to carry this work forward, in whatever way fits your life.

Built For Rebuilding

A closing message of hope, truth, and direction.

If you take nothing else from this book, take this: **You are not starting over. You are starting wiser.**

Starting over implies erasure. It suggests that everything before this moment was wasted, wrong, or meaningless. That is not true. What came before this moment matters. Even the collapse. Especially the collapse.

You carry forward experience, awareness, humility, discernment, and strength that did not exist before life broke open. You are not returning to zero. You are standing on ground that has been tested. Rebuilding is not regression. It is refinement.

What You've Learned Along the Way

◊ You've seen how collapse fractures identity before it ever disrupts circumstances.

◊ You've learned why dignity must come before strategy.

◊ You've been shown how clarity without shame creates stability instead of self-destruction.

◊ You've discovered that tools only work when they are simple, human, and grounded.

◊ You've learned that structure is not confinement, it is freedom.

◊ You've seen why income and stability are not selfish goals, but ethical ones.

And most importantly, you've learned this: **Rebuilding is not about becoming someone new. It is about becoming someone true.**

The Shift That Changes Everything

At the beginning of this journey, the question was likely: *"How do I fix my life?"* Somewhere along the way, that question evolved into something more honest: *"How do I rebuild a life that can actually hold me?"*

That shift matters.

Fixing implies something is broken beyond recognition. Rebuilding recognizes that something valuable still exists beneath the wreckage. You are not a problem to solve. You are a person to restore.

What Comes Next Is Not a Rush

Rebuilders often feel pressure to "catch up." To make up for lost time. To prove something. To justify survival. But rebuilding does not reward speed. It rewards steadiness. You now understand that:

• Consistency matters more than intensity

• Direction matters more than urgency

• Truth matters more than appearance

• Dignity matters more than approval

The next season of your life does not require performance. It requires alignment.

The Quiet Confidence of the Rebuilder

As you move forward, you may notice something subtle begin to change.

◊ You pause more before deciding.

◊ You choose clarity over chaos.

◊ You listen to your nervous system instead of overriding it.

◊ You build systems that support you instead of draining you.

◊ You stop chasing validation and start building stability.

That is wisdom taking root.

◊ You don't need to announce it.

◊ You don't need to defend it.

◊ You don't need permission.

Your life will speak for itself.

A Final Truth to Carry With You

You will face future challenges. That is not pessimism, it is reality. But you will face them differently now. With tools. With structure. With self-trust. With dignity intact.

You know how to rebuild. And that knowledge changes everything.

A Closing Invitation

As you close this book, I want to leave you with a final invitation.

Don't aim for perfection. Aim for honesty.

Don't aim to impress. Aim to stabilize.

Don't aim to erase the past. Aim to integrate it.

Build slowly.

Build truthfully.

Build with intention.

And when life shifts again, because it will, remember this:

You are not fragile.

You are not late.

You are not disqualified.

You are Built for Rebuilding.

And whatever comes next, you are ready to meet it, not because life will be easy, but because you now know how to rise without losing yourself. This is not the end of the work. It is the beginning of a wiser chapter...

And you don't have to walk it alone.

The Five Pillars of Built for Rebuilding™

A simple reference for rebuilding life, identity, and stability

B uilt for Rebuilding™ is not a collection of ideas. It is a system. At the center of that system are **five interconnected pillars** that guide every rebuild, regardless of where a person begins or what caused their collapse. These pillars are not stages you "complete." They are foundations you **strengthen over time**. Some rebuilders begin with identity work. Others begin with income or structure. But no rebuild holds unless **all five pillars are present**.

This appendix exists as a **reference point**, a way to orient yourself whenever the path feels unclear.

The Structure at a Glance

Center Pillar

1. Dignity & Identity Restoration

Four Corner Pillars

2. Truth & Clarity

3. Tools & Skill Building

4. Structure & Strategy

5. Income & Stability

Everything in this book, and everything within the Built for Rebuilding™ platform, fits inside this architecture.

Pillar 1 (Center): Dignity & Identity Restoration

What it is:

The restoration of worth, agency, and identity after collapse.

Why it comes first:

A person cannot rebuild a life they do not believe they deserve. Collapse fractures identity long before it damages circumstances. Shame, stigma, trauma, and failure erode dignity. Without restoring dignity, every other effort becomes fragile.

What this pillar restores:

- A sense of inherent worth
- The belief that the future is still possible
- Identity separate from collapse, labels, or mistakes
- The internal permission to rebuild without shame

Without this pillar:

People may survive, cope, or function, but they struggle to rebuild sustainably.

Pillar 2: Truth & Clarity

What it is:

The ability to see your life honestly, without distortion, denial, or self-attack.

Why it matters:

Rebuilding fails when people avoid the truth or punish themselves for it.

Truth & Clarity allow you to:

- Name what is real
- Separate facts from fear
- Take accountability without shame
- Make grounded decisions instead of reactive ones

This pillar includes:

- Honest self-assessment
- Trauma-aware reflection
- Calm accountability
- Clear decision-making

Without this pillar:

People rebuild on avoidance, blame, or false narratives, which eventually collapse again.

Pillar 3: Tools & Skill Building

What it is:

The practical capabilities required to rebuild daily life, work, and stability.

Why it matters:

Rebuilders don't need complexity. They need competence. This pillar focuses on **simple, usable tools** that rebuild confidence through action.

This pillar includes:

- Emotional regulation tools
- Communication skills
- Decision frameworks
- Planning basics
- Financial literacy
- Entrepreneurship and employment fundamentals

Without this pillar:

People know what they want but lack the skills to execute it, creating frustration and self-doubt.

Pillar 4: Structure & Strategy

What it is:

The systems and sequencing that turn effort into progress.

Why it matters:

Chaos is not a strategy.
Rebuilding without structure leads to:
- Burnout
- False starts
- Repeated collapse
- Emotional exhaustion
This pillar provides **order, pacing, and direction.**

This pillar includes:

- Clear sequencing (identity → clarity → stability)
- Planning systems
- Routines and rhythms
- Sustainable daily practices
- Long-term thinking without overwhelm

Without this pillar:

People work hard but remain stuck, scattered, or reactive.

Pillar 5: Income & Stability

What it is:

The economic and practical foundation that allows rebuilding to hold.

Why it matters:

Stability is not optional.

Without income and basic security:

- Stress overrides clarity
- Identity work cannot sustain itself
- Growth becomes fragile

This pillar supports **livable rebuilding**, not hustle culture.

This pillar includes:

- Employment pathways
- Entrepreneurship options
- Hybrid income strategies
- Financial grounding
- Long-term sustainability

Without this pillar:

Rebuilding becomes emotionally noble but practically unstable.

How the Five Pillars Work Together

The Five Pillars are not linear steps. They are **mutually reinforcing**.

- Dignity makes truth bearable
- Truth makes tools effective
- Tools require structure
- Structure supports stability
- Stability protects dignity

Every rebuilder moves through the pillars at their own pace, in their own order, but **no pillar can be ignored indefinitely**.

A Final Note for the Reader

If you ever feel overwhelmed, stuck, or uncertain, return here. Ask yourself:

- Which pillar feels weakest right now?
- Which pillar needs attention before I push forward?
- Where am I trying to skip ahead?

Rebuilding is not about speed. It is about integrity. This framework exists to help you rebuild **once**, and rebuild **well**.

The Rebuilder's Decision Framework

(6 Questions)

Move through these questions in order. Do not rush them. Write your answers when possible.

1. What is actually happening right now?

This is the truth question.

Strip away:

- Fear-based storytelling
- Shame narratives
- Catastrophic thinking
- Other people's expectations

Ask:

- What are the facts?
- What do I know for certain?
- What am I assuming?

Practice: Write one paragraph that begins with:

"Right now, the reality of my situation is…"

Clarity begins with accuracy, not emotion.

2. *What part of this is within my control?*

Collapse creates the illusion of helplessness.

This question restores agency. Ask:

- What can I influence today?
- What is not mine to control?
- Where am I wasting energy on outcomes I can't manage?

Practice: Divide a page into two columns:

- Within My Control
- Outside My Control

Decisions belong only in the first column.

3. What does my nervous system need in order to think clearly?

No good decision is made while dysregulated. Ask:

- Am I tired?
- Am I hungry?
- Am I activated, anxious, or overwhelmed?
- Am I reacting instead of responding?

If regulation is needed, pause the decision.

Practice: Use the 3-Breath Reset:

- Three slow breaths in through the nose.
- One long exhale through the mouth.

Then reassess.

Stability precedes clarity.

4. *Which pillar does this decision primarily affect?*

Every decision strengthens or weakens one of the Five Pillars. Ask:
- Is this an identity decision?
- A truth and clarity decision?
- A tools or skills decision?
- A structure decision?
- A stability or income decision?

Practice: Name the pillar out loud or in writing. Misplaced decisions create internal conflict. Aligned decisions create relief.

5. What is the smallest honest step forward?

Rebuilders often overreach. This question prevents burnout. Ask:
- What is the next *honest* step, not the impressive one?
- What would progress look like at 10%, not 100%?
- What action aligns with dignity and sustainability?

Practice: Complete this sentence:

"The smallest step I can take without betraying myself is…"

Small steps rebuild trust. Trust rebuilds momentum.

6. Will this decision support the life I am rebuilding, not just the moment I'm in?

This is the long-horizon question. Ask:
- Will Future Me thank me for this?
- Does this create stability or chaos?
- Does this move me toward alignment or away from it?

If the answer is unclear, slow down.

Practice: Ask:

"Does this decision help me build a life I can actually sustain?"
If not, revisit earlier questions.

When You're Stuck Between Two Options

Use this grounding comparison:

Option A:

- Supports dignity?
- Increases clarity?
- Preserves energy?
- Builds stability?

Option B:

- Supports urgency?
- Relieves anxiety temporarily?
- Creates pressure?
- Delays truth?

Choose the option that supports **long-term steadiness**, not short-term relief.

A Note on Mistakes

You will still make imperfect decisions. That does not mean you are failing. Rebuilding is iterative. Each decision teaches you more about yourself, your needs, and your capacity. The goal is not perfection. The goal is **alignment**.

A Closing Reminder

When life feels unclear, return to this framework. Not to overthink. Not to self-judge. But to slow the moment enough to choose with dignity.

You are allowed to:

- Pause
- Ask better questions
- Choose differently than before
- Decide without punishment

That is what rebuilding looks like in practice.

Worksheets for Truth, Clarity, Strategy, and Stability

How to use these tools without overwhelm or self-judgment

These worksheets are not tests. They are not assignments. They are not something you need to "get right." They exist for one reason: To help you **slow your thinking**, **organize your reality**, and **move forward without losing yourself**. Rebuilding does not require intensity. It requires steadiness. These worksheets are designed to create that steadiness.

How to Use This Appendix

You do not need to complete every worksheet at once. You do not need to move through them in order. You do not need to finish them perfectly. You only need to start where you are.

Each worksheet corresponds to one of four core rebuild areas:

- **Truth**: seeing what is real
- **Clarity**: understanding what matters now

- **Strategy**: choosing direction and sequencing
- **Stability**: creating a life that can hold your progress

If life feels overwhelming, start with **Truth**.

If you feel scattered, start with **Clarity**.

If you feel stuck, start with **Strategy**.

If you feel unstable, start with **Stability**.

Return to these tools whenever life gets loud again.

What These Worksheets Are Designed to Do

These tools help you:

- Separate facts from fear
- Reduce mental chaos
- Restore a sense of agency
- Make decisions without panic
- Build momentum through clarity
- Create structure without rigidity

They are intentionally simple. Rebuilders do not need complexity.

They need tools that work **when energy is low and emotions are high**.

What "Done" Looks Like

There is no finish line here. A worksheet is complete when:

- You feel clearer than when you started
- Your nervous system feels calmer
- One small next step becomes visible

If a worksheet raises emotion, pause.

If it brings clarity, stop there.

If it feels heavy, take a break.

Progress is measured by **stability**, not speed.

A Note on Shame and Self-Judgment

If you feel resistance, avoidance, or frustration while working through these pages, nothing is wrong. That resistance is information.

It often means:

- You're touching something real
- You're naming something you've avoided
- You're beginning to shift identity

Treat that resistance with curiosity, not criticism. These tools are meant to support you, not expose you.

How Often to Use These Worksheets

There is no prescribed schedule. Some rebuilders use one worksheet per week. Some return to the same worksheet for months. Some revisit them at major transition points.

Use them:

- When life changes
- When decisions feel heavy
- When clarity disappears
- When you feel yourself reacting instead of choosing

This appendix is a **resource**, not a requirement.

How These Worksheets Fit the Built for Rebuilding System

These worksheets are not separate from the book. They are extensions of it. Each worksheet reinforces:

- Dignity before pressure
- Truth before action

- Structure before urgency
- Stability before expansion

They are designed to work alongside the Five Pillars, not replace them.

One Final Reminder Before You Begin

You are not behind. You are not failing. You are not doing this "wrong." Rebuilding is not linear. It is lived. Use these pages as companions, not judges.

When you're ready, begin with the worksheet that matches your current need.

Truth Worksheets

Seeing what is real without distortion or collapse

Rebuilding begins with truth. Not harsh truth. Not self-attacking truth. Not the kind of "honesty" that leaves you feeling exposed or defeated.

This section is about **steady truth**.

Truth that stabilizes instead of overwhelms. Truth that clarifies instead of condemns. Truth that gives you something solid to stand on.

These worksheets help you name reality **as it is**, not as fear, shame, or pressure tells you it is.

How to Use the Truth Worksheets

Use these worksheets when:

- Your mind feels noisy or foggy
- You feel overwhelmed but can't explain why
- You're stuck in fear-based thinking
- You're avoiding a situation you know you need to face
- You feel pressure to "figure everything out" at once

You do not need to complete both worksheets in one sitting.

If energy is low, start with **Worksheet 1**. If something feels unspoken or heavy, move to **Worksheet 2**. Stop when clarity increases. That is the goal.

Truth Worksheet 1
Facts vs. Fear Snapshot

Purpose

This worksheet separates **what is actually happening** from **what your mind is adding** under stress. Collapse trains the brain to catastrophize. This tool brings you back to solid ground.

Instructions

Take one situation that feels heavy right now. Do not choose the biggest issue in your life. Choose the one that is currently consuming your attention. Write slowly. Short answers are enough.

SECTION A: Name the Situation

What situation am I reacting to right now? (Example: Job search, finances, relationship tension, legal issue, health concern)

_____

_____

SECTION B: The Facts (What I Know for Certain)

Write only what can be verified or observed. No assumptions. No predictions.

Examples:

- "I have submitted three applications."
- "My bank balance is $___."
- "I have not received a response yet."
- "I feel anxious when I think about this."

The facts are:

_____

_____

_____

_____

SECTION C: The Fear Story (What My Mind Is Adding)

This is the internal narrative running beneath the surface.

Examples:

- "I'm running out of time."
- "This proves I'm failing."
- "I'll never recover from this."
- "People see me as broken."

The fear story is:

_____

_____

_____

_____

SECTION D: Reality Check

Answer honestly:

- **Which parts of this are facts?**
- **Which parts are fear, prediction, or shame?**

What I am confusing with reality is:

_____

_____

_____

SECTION E: Grounded Reframe

Complete this sentence: "Based on the facts, the most honest way to describe my situation is…"

_____

_____

_____

_____

Next Step

Before taking action, pause.

Ask:

"What would I do next if I trusted the facts instead of the fear?"

Write one small step:

_____

_____

_____

_____

Truth Worksheet 2
What I'm Not Saying Yet

Purpose

Collapse often teaches silence. This worksheet helps you name:

- The truth you're avoiding
- The truth you're minimizing
- The truth you're afraid to admit, even to yourself

This is not about confession. It is about **relief**.

Instructions

This worksheet is private. No one else needs to see it. Write without editing yourself.

SECTION A: The Unspoken Truth

Complete this sentence honestly: "What I'm not saying out loud right now is…"

_____

_____

_____

SECTION B: What I'm Afraid Will Happen If I Admit This

Examples:

- "I'll feel weak."
- "I'll disappoint people."
- "I'll have to make a change."
- "I won't like the answer."

If I tell the truth, I'm afraid that:

_____

_____

_____

_____

SECTION C: What This Truth Is Asking of Me

Truth is not a punishment. It is information.

Ask:

- What boundary is needed?
- What decision is waiting?
- What support is missing?
- What needs to change?

This truth is asking me to:

_____

_____

_____

_____

SECTION D: The Compassion Check

Answer gently:

"If someone I cared about were facing this same truth, I would tell them…"

_____

_____

_____

_____

Now read that sentence back to yourself.

Next Step

Complete this sentence:

"The smallest honest step I can take after naming this truth is…"

_____

_____

_____

_____

Before You Move On

If you feel:

- Calmer
- Clearer
- Less reactive
- More grounded

You are done for now. You do not need to solve everything today. Truth stabilizes first. Action comes later.

Clarity Worksheet: Constraints and Options Map

Purpose

This worksheet helps you see your situation realistically **without turning limits into self-judgment**. Constraints are not failures. They are conditions. Rebuilders make better decisions when they understand both.

Instructions

Do not try to change anything yet. Simply name what exists.

SECTION A: Current Constraints

List the real limitations you are working within.

Examples:

- Time
- Money
- Health
- Legal restrictions

- Energy
- Caregiving responsibilities
- Location

My current constraints are:

_____

_____

_____

_____

SECTION B: What These Constraints Require (Not What They Mean)

Instead of interpreting constraints as identity statements, ask:

- What do these conditions require of me?
- What pace do they demand?
- What support do they make necessary?

These constraints require me to:

_____

_____

_____

_____

SECTION C: Available Options Within These Constraints

This is where agency returns.

Ask:

- What *can* I do from here?
- What options exist that I've been overlooking?
- What choices respect my limits instead of fighting them?

My realistic options right now include:

_____

_____

_____

_____

SECTION D: The Dignity Check

Answer this carefully: "Which option allows me to move forward without betraying my health, values, or stability?"

_____

_____

_____

_____

Next Step

Complete this sentence: "Given my reality, the most aligned option to explore next is..."

_____

_____

_____

Before You Move On

If you feel:

- Less scattered
- More focused
- Less rushed
- More grounded in reality

You've done enough for now. Clarity does not shout. It settles.

Strategy Worksheets

Turning clarity into a simple, sustainable plan

S trategy is not hustle. It is not intensity. It is not doing more. Strategy is **choosing a direction and sequencing your effort** so that progress becomes possible. After collapse, many rebuilders confuse strategy with urgency. They push hard in too many directions, hoping something will work.

This section exists to prevent that. You are not building a five-year plan. You are creating a **stable path forward**.

How to Use the Strategy Worksheets

Use these worksheets when:

- You know what matters but don't know how to move forward
- You feel ready to act but fear making the wrong move
- You want momentum without burnout
- You need structure, not pressure

Strategy works best when it is:

- Simple
- Honest
- Flexible
- Aligned with your current capacity

Strategy Worksheet
The 90-Day Rebuild Target

Purpose

This worksheet helps you define a **single, stabilizing aim** for the next 90 days. Ninety days is long enough to make progress. Short enough to stay realistic.

Instructions

This is not about achievement. It is about **stability and direction**. Choose one area that would most support your rebuild right now.

SECTION A: The Area I Am Rebuilding First

Examples:

- Income
- Employment
- Education
- Health
- Housing
- Emotional stability
- Skill development
- Legal stability

The area I am prioritizing for the next 90 days is:

_____

_____

_____

_____

SECTION B: What "More Stable" Would Look Like

Avoid perfection. Describe improvement, not completion.

Examples:

- "Consistent income, even if small"
- "A daily routine I can keep"
- "Reduced anxiety around finances"
- "Clear next steps instead of guessing"

In 90 days, more stability would look like:

_____

_____

_____

SECTION C: What This 90-Day Target Is *Not*

This protects you from overreach.

Examples:

- "This is not my final career."
- "This is not my forever plan."
- "This is not proof of success or failure."

This target is not:

_____

_____

_____

SECTION D: The One Outcome That Matters Most

Ask:

- What single outcome would reduce stress the most?
- What result would create breathing room?

The one outcome I am aiming for is:

_____

_____

_____

_____

Next Step

Complete this sentence: "For the next 90 days, my primary focus is to build stability by…"

_____

_____

_____

_____

Strategy Worksheet 2
The Rebuild Sequence Plan

Purpose

This worksheet turns your 90-day aim into a **simple sequence**. Rebuilding fails when everything feels equally important. Sequencing restores momentum.

Instructions

You will identify **three steps**, not ten.

Each step should feel doable, not impressive.

SECTION A: Step One (Stabilize First)

This step reduces chaos or stress.

Examples:

- Apply for benefits
- Update resume
- Create a daily routine
- Schedule medical or legal support
- Set a basic budget

Step One is:

_____

_____

_____

_____

SECTION B: Step Two (Build Capability)

This step increases skill, confidence, or capacity.

Examples:
- Take a course
- Practice an interview skill
- Build a small habit
- Learn a financial tool

Step Two is:

_____

_____

_____

_____

SECTION C: Step Three (Expand Carefully)

This step moves you slightly beyond your current position.

Examples:
- Apply for a role
- Pitch a service
- Commit to a schedule
- Begin a project

Step Three is:

_____

_____

_____

_____

SECTION D: The Pace Check

Answer honestly: "If I moved at this pace for 90 days, I would feel…"

_____

If the answer includes exhaustion or panic, simplify.

SECTION E: The Stability Anchor

Complete this sentence: "If everything feels overwhelming, I will return to…"

_____

_____

This becomes your grounding reference point.

Before You Move On

If you now feel:
- Less rushed
- More directed
- Clear about next steps
- Able to move without pressure

Your strategy is working. Strategy should **relieve pressure**, not add it.

Stability Worksheets

Building a life that can hold your progress

S tability is not the reward at the end of rebuilding. It is the condition that allows rebuilding to continue. Many people rebuild momentum but lose it because their life cannot support it. Stress spikes. Energy collapses. Old patterns return.

This section exists to prevent that.

Stability is not perfection. It is **enough structure, support, and predictability** to keep moving forward without burning out or falling apart.

How to Use the Stability Worksheets

Use these worksheets when:
- You feel fragile even though progress is happening
- You fear losing ground
- You're exhausted from "holding it together"
- You want your rebuild to last, not just work briefly

Stability is built quietly. These tools help you build it intentionally.

Resources for Justice-Impacted Rebuilders

Practical support for rebuilding with dignity, not charity

Rebuilding after justice involvement is not a mindset problem. It is not a motivation problem. It is not a character problem. It is a **systems problem** layered on top of personal recovery, identity repair, and survival.

This appendix exists to do three things:

1. Acknowledge the real barriers justice-impacted people face
2. Point to **credible, proven resources** that reduce those barriers
3. Reinforce a core truth of this book:

People do not fail at reentry. Systems fail to support it.

These resources are starting points, not guarantees. But access to the right tools, organizations, and information can radically change the trajectory of a rebuild.

How to Use This Appendix

Use this section if you are:

- Justice-impacted yourself
- Supporting someone navigating reentry
- Building programs, hiring pipelines, or partnerships
- Looking for legitimate help, not empty promises

You are encouraged to:

- Bookmark organizations
- Share this list
- Revisit it as your rebuild progresses

Section 1: National Reentry & Justice Reform Organizations

These organizations focus on **systemic reentry support**, policy advocacy, and practical services.

- **The Fortune Society**

  Comprehensive reentry services including housing, employment, mental health support, and advocacy.

- **Just Leadership USA**

  Leadership development and policy advocacy led by formerly incarcerated individuals.

- **Prison Fellowship**

  Reentry programs, family restoration, and support inside and outside incarceration.

- **The Marshall Project**

  Investigative journalism and data-driven reporting on the U.S. justice system.

- **Vera Institute of Justice**

  Research, policy reform, and system-level reentry initiatives.

Section 2: Employment & Workforce Development (Second-Chance Focus)

Stable income is not optional for rebuilding. These organizations focus on **real employment pathways**, not résumé theater.

- **Honest Jobs**

  Job board and employer network built specifically for justice-impacted job seekers.

- **Center for Employment Opportunities**

  Transitional jobs, job placement, and long-term employment support.

- **70 Million Jobs**

  Employment platform connecting employers open to hiring justice-impacted individuals.

- **Defy Ventures**

  Entrepreneurship training, business education, and leadership development for justice-impacted individuals.

Section 3: Education, Skill Building, and Entrepreneurship

Reentry without skill-building traps people in survival mode. These organizations focus on **capability, not charity**.

- **PEN America Prison Writing Program**

  Writing education, mentorship, and publication support for incarcerated and formerly incarcerated people.

- **Inmates to Entrepreneurs**

  Business education and mentorship for justice-impacted entrepreneurs.

- **The Last Mile**
  Technology and coding education designed for reentry-ready skills.

- **Edovo**
  Secure tablets and educational content for incarcerated individuals preparing for reentry.

Section 4: Mental Health, Trauma, and Recovery Support

Reentry without mental health support often leads to relapse, burnout, or recidivism. These resources respect trauma without pathologizing people.

- **National Alliance on Mental Illness**
  Education, peer support, and navigation resources for mental health care.

- **Substance Abuse and Mental Health Services Administration**
  Treatment locators, crisis resources, and recovery support programs.

- **Trauma Recovery Institute**
  Trauma-informed education and recovery frameworks.

Section 5: Legal Aid, Record Relief, and Rights Education

Legal barriers don't disappear after release. Knowing your rights is a stabilizing force.

- **National Reentry Resource Center**
  Centralized hub for reentry policies, tools, and technical assistance.

- **Legal Action Center**

  Resources on employment rights, discrimination, and record-based barriers.

- **Collateral Consequences Resource Center**

  Comprehensive information on record relief, expungement, and legal consequences by state.

Section 6: Housing & Reentry Stability

Housing instability is one of the strongest predictors of recidivism. These organizations work where the system often fails.

- **Returning Home Ohio**

  Housing-focused reentry support model.

- **Fortune Academy**

  Supportive housing specifically for justice-impacted individuals.

- **National Low Income Housing Coalition**

  Research and advocacy on housing access, including reentry barriers.

Section 7: A Note on Sidre

Some readers will want more than resources. They will want **structure, education, and sustained support**. That is why **Sidre** exists. Sidre is not a referral list. It is a **rebuild system** designed around:

- Business education
- Employment readiness
- Skill development
- Dignity-centered support
- Long-term stability, not short-term fixes

Sidre represents the heart of the Built for Rebuilding mission: **Reentry is not a favor. It is a responsibility.**

Closing Note for Appendix D

Justice-impacted rebuilders are not broken. They are navigating a system designed to make rebuilding harder than it should be. Access to the right resources does not guarantee success. But lack of access almost guarantees struggle. Use what helps. Ignore what doesn't. Advocate where you can. And remember:

Rebuilding with dignity is not a privilege… It is a human right.

Recommended Reading & Tools

A practical library for rebuilding
with dignity, clarity, and structure

Rebuilding requires more than belief. It requires **language, frameworks, and tools** that help you think clearly, act intentionally, and stay grounded when the work gets hard. This appendix is not a list of "inspirational" books. It is a **curated rebuild library**.

Each resource here earned its place because it does at least one of the following:

- Restores dignity instead of exploiting pain
- Encourages responsibility without shame
- Offers usable frameworks, not vague motivation
- Respects lived experience and complexity
- Supports long-term stability, not quick fixes

You do not need to read everything. Choose what meets you **where you are** in your rebuild. Take what serves you. Leave what doesn't. Return when the season changes.

Section 1: Identity, Dignity, and the Human Condition

These works explore meaning, worth, suffering, resilience, and the internal experience of being human in moments of collapse and rebuilding.

- **Man's Search for Meaning** – Viktor Frankl

  A foundational exploration of dignity, meaning, and agency in the face of suffering. Central to the philosophy of rebuilding without surrendering identity.

- **The Body Keeps the Score** – Bessel van der Kolk

  A critical understanding of how trauma lives in the body and why rebuilding requires more than cognitive effort.

- **Daring Greatly** – Brené Brown

  A guide to vulnerability, courage, and reclaiming worth after shame and failure.

- **The Gifts of Imperfection** – Brené Brown

  A practical and compassionate framework for letting go of who we think we're supposed to be and embracing who we are.

Section 2: Truth, Thinking, and Cognitive Clarity

These books sharpen awareness, challenge distorted thinking, and help rebuilders see reality clearly without self-attack.

- **Thinking, Fast and Slow** – Daniel Kahneman

  A deep dive into how the mind actually makes decisions, and why clarity requires understanding our cognitive blind spots.

- **Predictably Irrational** – Dan Ariely

  A powerful companion to truth and clarity work. It explains why humans behave irrationally in consistent ways, and how awareness of those patterns leads to better decisions, especially under stress and uncertainty.

- **You Are Not Your Brain** – Jeffrey Schwartz & Rebecca Gladding
  A practical guide to separating identity from intrusive thoughts and emotional reactions.

Section 3: Emotional Regulation, Resilience, and Mental Fitness

These resources support emotional steadiness, resilience without toxicity, and internal stability during rebuild seasons.

- **Emotional Intelligence** – Daniel Goleman
  A foundational text on self-awareness, emotional regulation, and relational competence.
- **Atomic Habits** – James Clear
  A practical framework for rebuilding identity through small, repeatable actions rather than willpower or motivation.
- **The Comfort Crisis** – Michael Easter
  Explores resilience, discomfort, and the role of intentional challenge in rebuilding strength without self-destruction.

Section 4: Leadership, Integrity, and Personal Standards

These books support rebuilding leadership, character, and internal operating principles, whether for self-leadership or leading others.

- **Extreme Ownership** – Jocko Willink & Leif Babin
  A disciplined approach to accountability and responsibility, useful when reframed through compassion rather than punishment.
- **The Obstacle Is the Way** – Ryan Holiday
  A modern application of Stoic philosophy that aligns with grounded, reality-based rebuilding.

- **Leadership and Self-Deception** – The Arbinger Institute
  A powerful exploration of how self-justification distorts truth and relationships.

Section 5: Strategy, Structure, and Sustainable Building

These works focus on building systems, plans, and structures that hold under pressure.

- **The Business Blueprint** – Joe Cullen
  A methodical, human-centered approach to planning and building work that aligns with identity, capacity, and sustainability. Included here because rebuilding requires structure without overwhelm.
- **Good Strategy / Bad Strategy** – Richard Rumelt
  A clear, no-nonsense guide to strategy that cuts through jargon and complexity.
- **Essentialism** – Greg McKeown
  A practical guide to doing less, better, especially valuable for rebuilders recovering from burnout or chaos.

Section 6: Reentry, Justice, and Second-Chance Realities

These resources speak directly to justice-impacted rebuilders and those committed to dignity-centered reentry and reform.

- **Reentry Matters** – Jenny Roberts
  A critical exploration of reentry challenges, systemic barriers, and why second chances require more than personal effort.
- **The New Jim Crow** – Michelle Alexander
  A foundational text for understanding how systems shape identity, opportunity, and long-term consequences after justice involvement.

- **Just Mercy** – Bryan Stevenson
  A deeply human account of justice, dignity, and the moral necessity of second chances.

Section 7: Purpose, Meaning, and the Long View

These books support rebuilding beyond survival, helping readers connect their rebuild to contribution and meaning.

- **Start With Why** – Simon Sinek
  A framework for aligning work and purpose once stability begins to return.
- **The Alchemist** – Paulo Coelho
  A symbolic and reflective reminder that rebuilding is as much about listening inward as it is about external progress.

Section 8: Practical Tools & Platforms

These tools support **execution, not overwhelm**.

- **Notion**
  Flexible workspace for rebuild plans, journaling, and systems.
- **Google Docs**
  Simple, accessible tools for planning and reflection.
- **Canva**
  Useful for resumes, presentations, and rebuilding professional identity.
- **You Need A Budget**
  A clear, behavior-based budgeting system aligned with stability.

A Final Note on Reading During Rebuild

You do not need to read all of these. You do not need to read them in order. You do not need to read them quickly. Rebuilding is not accelerated by consumption. It is strengthened by **integration**. One book at the right moment can change everything. Trust yourself to know which one that is.

About the Author

J oe Cullen is not an expert on rebuilding because he studied it from a distance. He is an expert because he lived it.

Over the course of his life, Joe has experienced multiple forms of collapse: personal, professional, psychological, and physical. He has rebuilt from public failure and private despair, from success and from stigma, from ambition and from ashes. *Built for Rebuilding* exists because Joe knows firsthand that rebuilding a life requires more than motivation. It requires dignity, structure, and a system that honors both reality and humanity.

Joe's story includes moments that few people speak openly about. He has faced legal trouble, arrest, and a felony conviction. He has experienced homelessness and the loss of identity that comes when the world reduces you to a label. He has battled undiagnosed bipolar disorder and severe, treatment-resistant depression for much of his adult life, including periods marked by suicide attempts and deep psychological crisis. He has navigated physical health challenges alongside mental illness, often while trying to lead, provide, and perform at a level the world expected but never asked how he was surviving.

These experiences were not abstract struggles. They were lived realities. They dismantled his sense of self, stripped away certainty, and forced him to confront the hardest truth of all: that intelligence, drive, and past success do not protect a person from collapse.

What ultimately allowed Joe to rebuild was not denial or bravado, but truth and structure.

For more than a decade, Joe has engaged in weekly therapeutic work rooted in Cognitive Behavioral Therapy (CBT), alongside deep study and application of Stoic philosophy and Human Design theory. These disciplines helped him understand how thought patterns, emotional regulation, identity, and decision-making shape outcomes over time. They also reinforced a core belief that runs throughout this book: rebuilding is not about becoming someone new, but about reclaiming who you are beneath survival, shame, and distortion.

Professionally, Joe brings extensive business and leadership experience to his work. He has served in corporate leadership roles, including as a Sales Director, and has founded five companies across media, operations, and services. Three of those companies were successfully exited through acquisition. The fourth, Race City Management: Sports and Entertainment, became his most visible and painful professional collapse, a fast-growing, high-profile venture that fell apart loudly and publicly, reshaping his career and identity.

The fifth company is his current rebuild.

Today, Joe operates at the intersection of lived experience and practical application. Through **Joe Cullen Ltd.**, he works with entrepreneurs, professionals, and leaders rebuilding careers, businesses, and identities after disruption, burnout, or reinvention. Through **Sidre**, a nonprofit organization he founded, Joe supports justice-impacted individuals navigating reentry, stigma, and systemic barriers to stability, work, and dignity.

Built for Rebuilding is the unifying framework behind both efforts.

Joe does not present rebuilding as a linear journey or a guaranteed outcome. He presents it as a disciplined, compassionate process rooted in truth, clarity, tools, structure, and stability. His work is grounded in the belief that people do not fail because they lack effort; they falter because they are asked to rebuild without a foundation.

Joe Cullen writes, teaches, and advises with one central conviction: Every person deserves the chance to rebuild a life stronger than the one that broke, and no one should have to do it alone.

www.ingramcontent.com/pod-product-compliance
Lightning Source LLC
Chambersburg PA
CBHW070908130626
46555CB00001B/42